Studying the Book of Amos

STUDYING THE BOOK OF AMOS

John D. W. Watts

BROADMAN PRESS

Nashville, Tennessee

DEWEY DECIMAL CLASSIFICATION: 224.8

Library of Congress catalog card number: 66-19904

Printed in the United States of America

5.D6513

Preface

These pages originated as lectures to theological students in Germany, Spain, and elsewhere. They are published in view of the projected study of Amos in Southern Baptist churches in 1967.

The study is planned to help in understanding Amos, his message, and his faith, and to help in building bridges of application of the truths he proclaimed to modern life. It makes no attempt to project a teaching or study plan.

The preacher or teacher who is looking for more extended homiletical application will do well to read Roy Lee Honeycutt, Jr., *Amos and His Message: An Expository Commentary* (Broadman). Serious students who seek a reasoned basis for positions taken in the present book will find help in this author's monograph *Vision and Prophecy in the Book of Amos* (Eerdmans). Further intensive help will be provided by the October, 1966, issues of two Southern Baptist theological journals, *The Review and Expositor* and *The Southwestern Journal*, which usually devote an issue to studies in depth of the biblical book chosen for study in the churches the following year.

This little book is written in the hope that it may contribute to a clearer understanding of, as well as a deeper commitment to, the word of God contained in the priceless book of Amos.

Contents

Introduction

The Prophetic Word

The superscription "the words of Amos" (1:1) marks this little book as a prophetic book containing the messages of a certain Amos. The short speeches, which in Hebrew are called "words," were born in the heat of spiritual experiences with Amos' God. They present God's warnings and his call to repentance.

"Word" is the expression used more often than any other in the Old Testament for prophetic speech. The Hebrew root used here can also be translated "a thing." That which is described with this word is the revelation of God through his prophet. When spoken, these "words" not only inform but also call. They pronounce judgment and help to effect it. They show the day of salvation and make salvation a reality. When the prophet is caught up in the power of the Spirit, he stands high above any earthly power, fearlessly announcing his message which, for his people, means both judgment and salvation.

In this sense—that the prophetic word means both God's revelation and his salvation—we can much better understand the "Word become flesh" (John 1) in which the third characteristic of the word of God, its creative power, is also apparent. God as

Revealer, Redeemer, and Creator worked through his prophets in giving his word to his people. Amos was such a prophet and his "words" were of this kind.

Shepherd of Tekoa

These words remind us that prophetic literature is not simply interested in presenting the messages of the prophets. Their person and life are also important, for God's message is personally related and presented. He sends it through his elect messenger. It is, therefore, good to know who these men were. This necessary knowledge is passed on to us in short biographical accounts in the prophetic books. All that is known concerning Amos is found in this verse and in the story of his being driven out of Bethel (7:10-17).

Tekoa was a tiny village on the edge of the wilderness of Judah. This high plateau is hilly and cut by deep gorges. From the time of David until today, this wilderness has served as a hiding place for many a person seeking refuge. The manuscripts which were recently found in the caves of this region testify that in the time of Christ the sect of the Essenes had secret places of meeting in this territory.

Amos is described as a shepherd (or an owner of sheep and goats) who was also a tender of sycamore trees. Whatever this last profession is remains a mystery, but it is certain from these words that Amos was not "one of the prophets" in the normal sense of the word. He was a very ordinary man from the mountains and from the country, whose regular profession had to do with cattle and grass and trees.

Amos came from that quiet back country of Judah, which remained largely untouched by the progress of civilization. In these areas men lived the simple life of their fathers. They held fast to the faith which they knew to have been given them by Moses. Here every man was a complete man, free and independent, friendly and good to his guest, but vengeful and fearful toward anyone whom he had reason to call his enemy. In this place where everyone had to fight in order to wring from the desert his living, no one doubted God's strict laws and the immediate judgment which followed upon disobedience. God's rule and the moral law, according to which everyone who sinned reaped the fruit of sin, were equally as clear and obvious to the men who lived in this area as they had been to Moses, Samuel, Nathan, Ahijah, and Elijah in their times.

The tremendous rise of the Davidic empire in Jerusalem, along with all the glory and corruption which accompanied it, made little impression upon this part of the country. Throughout the whole history of Judah one can trace a clear division between the people of Jerusalem who were largely the descendants of those already in Jerusalem when David took over the city, not originally Israelites, and those "people of the land" who dwelled in the rest of Judah. Amos, like Micah, belonged to the latter group, unspoiled by the worldly ways of the capital city.

That Amos was a rough countryman should not be misunderstood. Amos lacked neither culture nor understanding. It may very well have been that he could neither read nor write, but his original power and perfection of expression and style revealed a polished poet and storyteller. Even today, there appears from time to time among the seminomadic peoples such a genius who has no idea of written language. The style of Amos is one of an original genius. His Hebrew had a robust perfection which can hardly be found anywhere else in the Old Testament. And his cry of moral indignation bears the rough power of the simple countryman whose conscience and feelings are not burdened with the syllogistic relativism of his more cultivated city neighbors.

Through all the history of the kingdoms there had existed in the back country of Judah a direct and original worship of Yahweh, uncorrupted by the influence of Baalism and its moral relativism. Amos was from such an environment. He must have appeared very uncultivated to the sophisticated elite of Samaria. His clothing and his manner made him stand out in any crowd as a simple Judean herdsman. He did not act like the average prophet who had been trained for proper service in one of the prophetic schools, who quite accurately might call himself "one of the prophets" (v. 14). His face and his hair bore the marks of the desert wind and sun. His eyes were accustomed to searching the far horizons for dangers which might threaten his flock, just as they were used to searching the sheep for signs of wounds or illness. His hands were skilled and marked by the heavy work of gathering sycamore figs.

The Call to Prophesy

We are not told in detail of Amos' call to be Yahweh's prophet. In reply to the command of the high priest he protested against being classified simply as one of the temple prophets who cowed under the priest's commands: "Yahweh took me from following the flock, and the Lord Yahweh said to me, 'Go, prophesy to my people Israel.' "

We can only imagine that desert scene. The knowledge of God which Amos displays was not born in a night. He was a man of deep convictions which had been wrought out of the hard experiences of life and upon which his life had been based—convictions which became articulate in the meditations of hours alone with his herds in the quiet desert.

Amos was not the first shepherd to be used of God. Among the patriarchs there was Jacob, and then Moses, then David, and now Amos. Each in his own way and place had been led to the "mountain of God." For each of these the tranquility of shepherd life was a preparation for the intensely demanding ministry to which God called them.

Somewhere there in the Judean desert the overwhelming conviction of God's call settled upon Amos. The directness of the call was similar to the call of Abraham, and Amos' response was just as direct and immediate. In telling of his call, Amos needed only to recite the command; his response was taken for granted as he turned directly to his task in proclaiming to the priest of Bethel the word of the Lord.

The dominating theme of Amos' faith was his knowledge of God as his absolute Lord. Once he was sure that God was actually calling, there could be no hesitation or wavering response. If the Lord said, "Go!" he must go. If Yahweh said, "Speak!" he must speak (cf. 3:8).

Just so, Amos abruptly and directly arranged his affairs and took up his ministry. The period of his actual ministry in Israel must have been rather short. One writer has maintained that he made only one speech, which lasted less than half an hour. This is certainly extreme and does not do justice to the information we have in the book. A period of two or three years would be adequate, though it may very well have been longer. At least three appearances at the autumn festival seem to be recorded.

Amos contains the three basic literary forms of which our prophetic books are composed: prophetic oracles (or better, messages), biographical accounts of the prophets written in the third person, and autobiographical accounts in the first person. We find indications of all three forms in the superscription to the book.

The Two Books of Amos

It must seem a little strange to the observant reader that we have here "The words of Amos . . . which he saw." It is true that there is at least one other occurrence of this combination (Hab. 1:1, "The oracle of God which Habakkuk the prophet saw"). But the ordinary word combination is "the word which came to Amos," or "the vision which Amos saw." How is it that here we have the two combined or mixed?

We will notice evidence of this combination of different prophetic forms throughout the book. In chapters 1-6 only direct messages are to be found, while the fundamental outline of chapters 7-9 is formed by autobiographical accounts of visionary experiences with a short biographical section added in chapter 7 and more messages of the prophet in chapters 8 and 9. It is obvious that the character of the two parts is quite different, forming *two* books of Amos which have been combined.

The Book of Words.—The first book (chaps. 1-6) might quite appropriately bear the title "The Words of Amos." The messages deal entirely with conditions in the Northern Kingdom and may very well have been remembered and recorded there by a close friend or convert of the prophet. They were first preserved and transmitted by prophetic circles during the short years before the fall of Samaria. In that turbulent time many books were brought into the land of Judah by the men who had treasured them. The material of Deuteronomy, as well as that of the prophet Hosea, must have been among those materials so brought in. This part of Amos would have moved south with them.

The Book of Visions.—The second book of Amos (chaps. 7-9) is based on a series of visions. These are correctly viewed as accounts of real experiences of the prophet. It was through these experiences that the prophet's convictions and messages were formed.

The visions mark periods of time in the prophetic ministry of Amos. Together they form a short autobiography. Each vision characterizes one of these periods, while the prophetic messages give us the products of that period.

An exact description of the *Sitz im Leben* ("place in life")— the situation in which the accounts were spoken and repeated— eludes us. They must have been related at some occasion when the prophets and the friends of prophets gathered to reminisce and remind each other of the great speeches of the prophets. There Amos would have recounted his call and the visions which had formed his message. There he would have repeated his conviction that his message was true and still must be fulfilled. Perhaps he broke out into new oracles in support of the original prophecies.

This would mean that these accounts look on his ministry in retrospect. The account of his expulsion from Bethel is rightly placed after the third vision, for this third vision is the basis for his message of doom over Bethel. It was after this, when Amos was back in Judah, that these visions were recounted, remembered, repeated, and finally written into a book. It was in Judah that the Book of Visions came into being. It may quite appropriately have borne the title "The Visions of Amos Which He Saw Concerning Israel."

This may explain why the first three visions are not followed by messages. The messages delivered in these phases of his ministry were gathered and kept in Israel and were, therefore, not available to those who gathered this Book of Visions. On the other hand, the last two visions reflect phases of his ministry after his return to Judah. These messages were known to the Judean compiler, so they were naturally included under the accounts of the visions

The transmission of the Book of the Words came first through followers in northern Israel, while the Book of Visions had its home in Judah from the beginning. A period of oral transmission for both of them is probable for a short period, but there is no reason to suppose that this period lasted more than a few years. The two books in written form may have enjoyed separate existence for a much longer period. Their union was accomplished by simply putting them together and combining their superscriptions. This latter process may well be related to the collection of the twelve Minor Prophets. Since this compilation includes books certainly as late as the fifth century and there is no sure date for its completion before the fixing of the prophetic canon shortly before 200 B.C., this joining of the two parts of Amos may well have been in the postexilic era.

There is, however, no reason to question the authenticity of either section of the book. An anonymous scholarly scribe noted their identity and effected their happy union.

Israel

"Concerning Israel" might also be translated "against" or "upon Israel." The direct threat of impending judgment, which characterizes these prophecies, makes the latter translation more probable.

Israel means here the Northern Kingdom of Israel. The history of this little kingdom had been closely connected with prophetic activity from its very inception. It was at the suggestion of the prophet Ahijah (1 Kings 11:29 ff.) that Jeroboam I revolted against Rehoboam to set up the separate kingdom of the ten tribes.

The revolt was made possible by Egypt's pressure and finally through her intervention.

Once established in office, Jeroboam lost little time making his country independent of all ties to Judah and Jerusalem. Since these ties were basically religious, Jeroboam attempted to revive old traditions which antedated the work of David and Solomon in Jerusalem. He reestablished national shrines at the old sanctuaries at Dan and Bethel. In place of Jerusalem's ark with the cherubim, he chose a symbol which may well have been in common use in northern Israel at a much earlier date. Yahweh was symbolized as standing invisibly on the back of a bull (cf. Ex. 32). In theory this image was no more idolatrous than was that of the cherubim in Jerusalem. But in practice the symbol could be (and was) easily identified by the people with many features of Canaanite Baal worship. The priesthood of Dan laid claim to Mosaic origin (cf. Judg. 17-18), while that at Bethel may have laid claim to Aaron as their father. The energetic denial of this association by the Jerusalem priests has obscured the support for this claim.

Canaanite Culture

Solomon had opened up the entire realm to Canaanite influence, the fundamental culture of the land long before the Israelites came. In the united kingdom many Canaanite practices had
been brought into the court and even into the Temple. This
paganizing influence grew steadily in Israel.

In judging the frequent triumphs of Canaanite polytheism in Israel,
we must always bear in mind that polytheism had a popular appeal
in many ways like that of the dominant secularism of our own day.
The wealth, science and aesthetic culture of that age were lined up
on the side of Canaanite religion, thanks to the unprecedented progress
made by the great Phoenician cities and their smaller counterparts on
the coastal plain of Palestine. Compared with Phoenicia, the lands of
Judah and Israel were very poor, very rustic and far behind the spirit
of the day in fashions, arts of civilization, and material pleasures of
life. All the sinister fascination of the elaborate protosciences of magic
and divination was marshalled in defence of polytheism against the
stern, almost savage, simplicity of Mosaic theology.[1]

In contrast to the stability of the Davidic line in Judah, Israel's
kings led an uneasy life. Jeroboam was not able to pass on a firm
tenure in office to his son who was assassinated within two years
of ascending the throne. There followed a series of short reigns
which usually ended in assassination. Finally a general named
Omri was able to gain control (ca. 876 B.C.). These years of inner
turmoil left Israel weak; it is no wonder that she lost some of the
territory which had been firmly within Solomon's control.

Omri's Dynasty

Omri was strong enough to consolidate Israel's frontiers again.
It was he who began to build Israel's new capital which was to
be called Samaria. Omri's strength was sealed by alliances with

------

[1]W. F. Albright, "The Biblical Period," *The Jews: Their History, Culture,
and Religion,* ed. Louis Finkelstein (New York: Harper & Bros., 1949), p. 37.

Phoenicia and other Mediterranean states and cities. This policy helped bring stability and economic prosperity to the new country and was marked by the marriage of Omri's son Ahab to Jezebel, a princess of Tyre. This alliance was certainly formed to offset the increasing strength of Aram (Syria), but the resulting influx of Phoenician (Canaanite) culture and religion was to prove fatal to the dynasty of Omri.

In Ahab's reign (*ca.* 853) the Assyrian king Shalmaneser III moved against Aram. In the battle at Qarqar, Israel and Hamath stood with Aram against the Assyrians. The battle was apparently indecisive. The Assyrians withdrew and did not return for some five years. A later war between Aram and Israel accounted for the death of Ahab.

Parallel developments affected internal conditions in Israel. The opening of Israel's doors to the cultural and commercial influences of Phoenicia brought a great influx of religious influence as well. The Phoenician princess brought to Israel's palace her worship of the Tyrian gods Melkarth and Asherah. When a nation's influence was great, the number of worshipers of that nation's gods was correspondingly great. Phoenicia stood at the peak of her influence and her gods were worshiped everywhere within the radius of her power.

Israel was no exception. The domestic baalistic practices which had remained in the background for more than a century moved forward to identify themselves with the worship now actively espoused and propagated by the royal house.

Elijah

This development challenged the old Yahwistic faith as never before. The champion whom God raised up for that hour was Elijah. He seems to have been a rustic countryman from Gilead. Little is known about his person, but his deeds are written unforgettably in a short but glorious chapter of Israel's history (1 Kings 17-22; 2 Kings 1-2). He identified himself unmistakably with Mosaic Yahwism and challenged the position of Baalism in the land by announcing a great drought and then by provoking the contest on Mount Carmel. His challenging words, "If Yahweh is God, follow him," stand beside Joshua's command, "Choose you this day whom you will serve," as the most searching calls for faithful obedience in Israel's history.

But Elijah's battle was not only against the religious evils of Baalism. This new development threatened to undermine the basic structure of Israel's society through the establishment of a privileged aristocracy who felt themselves to be above the common demands of justice to the working peoples. When Elijah met Ahab in Naboth's vineyard, he was taking a stand against this development as well. Prophetic support of the just cause of the poor and lowly is at least as old as the days of Ahijah's rebellion against the oppressions of Solomon and his son, and of Samuel's warning to Israel concerning the possible evils of kingship.

Having clearly drawn the battle lines against Baalism through these incidents, Elijah prepared for the rout of the Tyrian Baal from Israelite soil. His methods were three: provision for continued prophetic power through Elisha's succession to his office; provision for the overthrow of the Omride dynasty and the elimination of their sponsorship of Baalism; and finally, the disruption of Israel's close ties to heathen nations through the accession of a strong and ambitious ruler to the throne of Aram.

The revolution which followed is described in detail. There was ample material to feed the fires of revolt. A volatile mixture of righteous indignation and religious fanaticism destroyed the worshipers of Baal and banished Melkarth and Asherah from Israel. Sustained economic unrest among the oppressed and abused new peasant classes, heightened by the disastrous drought of Ahab's day, exploded against the aristocratic landlords of the royal court. The final decisive element of revolution was provided by dissatisfied army officers who were restive under the weak foreign policy of the crown.

Jehu's Reign

Jehu's revolt swept Israel clean by a mighty blood bath (*herem*). But the new rulers were too weak and shortsighted to provide the leadership which might have reaped positive results from the revolt. The prophetic movement which had provided the incendiary stuff for revolution proved pitifully inadequate to the task of positive reconstruction. Stripped by the revolution of her former friends, Judah and Phoenicia, Israel now lay helpless before the attacks of Aram. Finally a crushing defeat by Assyria (805 B.C.) reduced Aram's superior strength and paved the way for the return of Israel's material fortunes in the eighth century.

Jeroboam II, fourth king in the dynasty of Jehu, reigned over Israel from 786 to 746 B.C. His father, Joash, waged successful wars against the weakened Aramean rulers and thus recovered most of the territory lost to them. The further happy circumstance that Assyria was not strong enough during the first half of the eighth century to assert its power in the West allowed Israel to recoup its power, wealth, and prestige. Never had Israel been so prosperous nor the standard of living so high.

In spite of this, all was not well in Israel. New prosperity increased disparity between rich and poor. Older standards of social and economic justice relaxed before the encroachment of Canaanite practices and corruptions. Although the Tyrian Melkarth had been deported a century before, the domestic baals that had dominated this soil long before Israel's appearance made a determined comeback. In some instances they were identified with Yahweh worship. In others Baal worship was gaining the upper hand on its own. Recent excavations from this period show as many names formed with Baal as with Yahweh.

There grew up a class of wealthy traders and landowners whose wealth and extravagance rivaled that of the king himself. There was no luxury or dainty which could not be secured in Samaria at this time. Palaces were expanded and magnificent mansions were built on all sides.

But this very prosperity was a sign of a great change in the social order. Israel had ceased to be a nation of small landowners. The moneylender had become a familiar person (cf. 2 Kings 4:1-7) in the land. When debts could not be paid, the land was forfeited. The former owner became the tenant, working land he no longer owned and receiving only a small share of the harvest.

When the demands upon him became too high, he went in debt again and had to sell his sons or even himself into slavery to pay. The order of society made up of free men owning their own land was rapidly disappearing, and with its disappearance the vitality and hardiness, the ability and morale of the fighting nation were removed. The history of Israel illustrates the fact that nations in that part of the world at that time could not survive without constant battle. The process of decay had been hastened by illegal practices and by the corruption of justice. The society was rotten at the heart, for all its seeming prosperity.

When Amos appeared on the scene, between 760 and 750 B.C. (the eclipse of the sun to which he refers was probably that of June 15, 763 B.C.), his eyes took in the situation with acute observation. He understood his prophetic mission to be that of announcing the destruction which was inevitable.

The trouble in the land was not that the people were irreligious. Quite the contrary. They paid the tithe scrupulously. They brought their sacrifices in abundance and observed all the feasts. Their religion was a syncretized mixture of Baal practices done in the name of Yahweh. Although the official political religion of Baal had been driven out a century before, the sanctuaries at Bethel, Gilgal, Beer-sheba, and even Jerusalem had made little improvement. Yahweh was worshiped as the old Canaanite Baal.

Most of the people probably felt that they were worshiping Yahweh. The tremendous failure of the religion was that it had been emptied of moral content. Worship and ethics had been divorced. The religious leaders could do nothing to prevent the moral and social decay of the country. Immorality had crept into the heart of the worship itself with sacred prostitution in the temples. Acts of worship were used to support the very acts of dishonesty and injustice. It is against the background of this scene that the words of Amos must be understood.

Social Contrasts

Another observation is pertinent to the understanding of Amos. The society just described was agricultural and had succumbed to the corruption of a heathen society and religion.

Amos represents a different society—the pastoral. In the southern and eastern parts of Palestine men lived by tending flocks and herds, much as they had since the time of the occupation. They maintained the same traditions and the same spirit and standards as had their fathers. Their view of life was quite different from that of the agricultural community. The moral requirements of God stood at the heart of their life; and at the heart of this religious understanding lay the requirement that man be just to his fellowmen. It is no wonder that the sights of the Northern Kingdom evoked such horror from Amos.

There were others, of course, who shared the background and the feeling of Amos, specifically the Rechabites and the Nazarites. But their response to the situation was quite other than his. They saw the horrors of civilization and shrank from them. They isolated themselves and would have nothing to do with them.

Amos did not want to do away with culture and civilization as such. He presented the demands of God that men be just and righteous as God is just and righteous. They must seek God rather than the sanctuaries if they were to live.

It was Amos' emphasis upon the ethical character of God and God's demands on men that was the distinctive point of his message. He did not present his message as something entirely new. This understanding must have been part of the original understanding of God's will within the covenant which went back to Moses. But it was the preaching of the prophets which lifted it again to make it the flag by which the people of God were to be recognized, the standard which should become the test of religion. Jesus did not hesitate to identify himself with this conviction and this concept of religious meaning.

Dates of Amos' Ministry

"Two years before the earthquake." This simple chronological note is the most exact dating given in the book of Amos. For contemporaries and persons living within the following decades it was certainly sufficient. That earthquake must have been great enough to stand out significantly, even in that land of frequent tremors.

Zechariah 14:5 refers to such an earthquake in the days of Uzziah. Josephus records a tradition (parallel to 2 Chron. 26) that a mighty earthquake rent Jerusalem on the same day that Uzziah usurped the place of the high priest in the rites of the Temple. The traditions seem to coincide with the vision of chapter 3 in Amos. Recent reconstruction of the events seems correct in placing this earthquake on New Year's Day of Jotham's accession year, 750 B.C. The date for Amos' famous speech in Bethel and his expulsion from the Northern Kingdom is then properly 752 B.C., two years before.

There is, however, no reason to assume that Amos' short speech at Bethel was the only one of his career in Israel. If the sketch of Amos' ministry, drawn from the accounts of his visions, is accurate, his work must have lasted at least several months and was more likely to have been about two years. It covered at least the years 754 B.C. to New Year's Day 752 B.C. in Israel before his expulsion from Bethel, and two full years before the earthquake, 752 to 750 B.C., in Judah. There is no way to determine the end of Amos' labors. He may have lived to see Israel's political structure crumble under the rod of God's anger like the buildings in his last vision (9:1-4).

Part I

THE MESSAGE OF AMOS

1

Vision of the Locusts

The First Period (7:1-3)

The Lord Yahweh.—The double name for God is typical of the visions. Its repeated and peculiar appearance here is in keeping with the more intimate nature of this part of the book and reveals much in regard to Amos' relationship to God.

The use of the personal covenant name for God, Yahweh, is to be found throughout the book. It is indicative that Amos stands in direct succession to all those who have been loyal to the original revelation through Moses. The name carries overtones that hint of the meaning of covenant and law, of election and deliverance, of promise and fulfilment. It stands for basic concepts of faith, of the relationship between God and his people, of judgment and salvation. "Yahweh" sums up the essential content of Mosaic and prophetic faith.

But it is the combination with "Lord" which makes this usage distinctive here. There is no other word which so adequately expresses Amos' fundamental concept of and relation to God. Yahweh was to him, above all, Lord: Lord over Amos and his message; Lord over Israel, her life, and her election; Lord over the nations; and Lord over the end. It is this deep conviction of Yahweh's supreme lordship which gives the messages of Amos power and authority. His faith and his theology will never be understood by anyone who has not first grasped this basic tenet of Amos' faith and experience.

Showed me.—The word used here to tell what God did for Amos is not the technical word for prophetic vision, which is found in the superscription. It is the causative form of the simple word "to see." "The Lord Yahweh caused me to see," says Amos. It is quite unnecessary for us to argue whether these visions involved material objects which the prophet saw, or whether they were dream visions. What is absolutely clear is that God dominated his thinking. Amos' attention fastened on a particular thing or happening, and he understood it to be a sign of God's coming judgment.

Amos was convinced that God had shown him this thing and had given him this interpretation of it. These experiences, then, become the turning points in Amos' ministry. They indicate the theme of his preaching for a period, until God speaks to him anew. In other words, what is told us here as one experience is not to be understood as finished in a few minutes. It is rather a condensed account of God's message to him and of his conversation (experience) in relation to this revelation which is given to him. In these first two visions we can clearly note God's assurance that his original decision has been changed. Not so with the final three in which the judgment is simply confirmed and intensified from one to the other. The visions are then a means of characterizing Amos' walk with God in a particular phase of his ministry.

The form.—At a glance, we see that the visions are presented in a form which is repeated again and again. The full form appears only in the accounts of the first two visions. The others move into a record of prophetic messages instead of continuing the account of the prophet's conversation with God. As we shall see, there is good reason for this change. But for the moment, let us analyze the form of these first two visions.

The first element is an introductory formula: "The Lord Yah-weh showed me," or, "I saw." The second element describes the thing seen. In the first two visions no explanation is required. The meaning is obvious. In the third and fourth the explanation is introduced with the question: "What do you see?" (Cf. visions in Jer., Ezek., and Zech. 4-5.) This serves to intensify the particular focus of the vision. Then the Lord gives the interpretation.

The next element in visions one and two is Amos' plea of intercession. This is a part of the prophetic ministry which is little understood and less emphasized. Let it suffice to note here that intercession is a part of the prophetic office, as well as that of the priest. The final element is the answer to the prophet's prayer.

This form is clear enough to demand an explanation. Where was it spoken and repeated? On what occasions? First, we should note that these accounts of a vision in the last three instances lead up to a proclamation of a new prophetic message. This would indicate that they were used as an introduction which helped explain and authenticate the message that followed.

This may well have been true of the first two visions at an earlier time. Our present rendering of them, however, comes on the occasion when the third or the fourth vision is the basis for Amos' current prophecy. The review of earlier prophetic experiences explains that they were not immediately and literally fulfilled, but have been succeeded by this later revelation.

A very convincing argument has been made for taking Amos' appearances at Bethel with the message contained in the third vision as falling on the occasion of the New Year's festival. If that is true, there is no reason for seeking further for the home of all these accounts. They are integral parts of the prophet's message, delivered at one or another of the great sanctuaries or gathering places on the occasion of a great festival—the first three in Israel, the final two in Judah.

Natural calamity, a portrait of judgment.—What Amos saw in the first vision was locusts. Perhaps he was walking through a field when his attention was drawn to locusts in a formative stage. Immediately recognizing the dire consequences of their presence, he understood that God would use them to punish Israel for her sin.

We have no record of prophetic messages concerning a plague of locusts, although other prophets have expounded this theme. There is no reason to date any of the messages of Amos in this period. But in 4:6-11 there is an interesting review in retrospect of a series of calamities which had befallen Israel. They were intended to chastise the people and turn them back to God.

It is a normal prophetic function to interpret such events for the people so as to lead them to repentance, that they might receive again God's blessings. The plague of locusts which Amos was given to see was such a calamity.

Amos may well have proclaimed this plague of locusts throughout Israel, urging the people to repent and turn back to Yahweh. His message may have centered in other catastrophes that are recorded in 4:6-11 as well. These include famine, droughts, plant diseases, plagues, as well as earthquake and volcanic eruptions like that of Sodom and Gomorrah.

What the immediate response to these messages was is not told us. We might gather from chapter 4 that the response was not lasting, to say the least. Repentance, if there was any at all, was shallow and soon forgotten. Repentance occasioned by the threat of natural calamity was not enough to bring about a real change of character in this people.

Prophetic intercession.—The account in the visions seems to point to at least enough response on the part of the people for the prophet to plead with God on their behalf (after the locusts had devoured all vegetation in the land):

O Lord Yahweh, forgive, I beseech thee!
How can Jacob stand?
He is so small! (RSV)

The cry is one for mercy, using the intimate name Jacob instead of Israel. God's people are weak and helpless. Only through God's mercy can they live. God's response is to change the decree that would have let just punishment descend on the people.

Amos is known as a preacher of judgment. He is that. But we do him an injustice if we think of him simply as a stern sadist who draws mean pleasure from his words of doom. As he fulfils his prophetic duty in delivering the dire prophecies of coming judgment, his heart is torn by his love and concern for this people of God. Amos reflects the bitter pathos in the Lord's words during the recital of the judgments which came on Israel, "Yet you did not return to me."

No preacher can properly thunder a message of sin and judgment to his people, nor effectively plead for repentance and changed life, whose heart does not bleed with them in their sufferings and whose lips fail to use every moment of private prayer for fervent intercession for them. Amos can be our model in this regard.

When the preacher presents his message of judgment without flinching, and passionately intercedes without ceasing, more often than not he may rise from his knees with a confident answer from the Lord, "It shall not be!"

2

Judgment by Fire

The Second Period (7:4-6)

Supernatural judgment.—The second vision begins like the first. But there is no natural object here to which the prophet's attention is called. Quite the contrary. He is led to understand that Yahweh is calling for "a judgment by fire."

This is no ordinary forest or grass fire. It is fire from heaven, a supernatural fire, which devours water as well as land. The fire which came from heaven to devour Elijah's altar, along with his well-soaked wood and the water around, was a tiny illustration of such fire. The fire which consumed Nadab and Abihu (Lev. 10:2) was another example of such fire.

The fire which Amos proclaims is one with tremendous, if not unlimited, destructive power. Its powers are not limited to this world; it devours "the great deep." This is not simply the ocean, it is the great and mystic ocean that, according to the ancient concept, surrounded the entire universe and was the home of the chaotic powers. This great judgment fire is capable of consuming all this. How much more the little land and people of Israel!

What Amos sees here is the clear indication of the judgment associated with the "Day of Yahweh." We may see in the mes-

sages of this period his development of this basic theme. But we
do well to note here that the judgment symbolized by this fire
is swift destruction without distinction of person or group. It is
indeed the instrument of the Lord's overflowing anger.

It is on the basis of this awful, overwhelming judgment that
Amos cries out his plea of intercession, before which God gives
way in gracious and merciful patience. This judgment had been
directed against Israel as a whole, without discriminating particular guilt. It gives way to the judgment of the following vision
where the guilt is specifically pointed out and the objects of
judgment are named.

Chapters 1-3 contain messages which seem appropriate to this
period. Particularly in the address contained in chapters 1-2 do
we find frequent references to a judgment by fire. This gives us
a positive link to the second vision. These messages may well
belong to the year before Amos is expelled from Bethel and
probably center in that New Year's Day previous to his final
appearance at Bethel.

It was on this New Year's Day that the people awaited the
"day of Yahweh." Some may have thought of it in the Canaanite
fashion as an annual occurrence in which God made all things
new again. Others certainly thought about it in an eschatological
fashion as the day on which Yahweh would fulfil all his promises
of power and glory to his people. It seems that almost no one
had thought of it in terms of judgment on Israel as well as
on the nations, as Amos proclaimed it.

Seven National Judgments (1:2 to 2:16)

Our record of the "words" of Amos begins by presenting a
full address from his mouth, perhaps the only complete one
extant. Most of the book is composed of isolated "words" or
messages of the prophet which could in actual use be presented
individually or grouped to form a larger whole as this first speech
so well shows.

This speech is composed of an introductory "word," followed by eight words of judgment addressed to eight different nations. We have every reason to suppose that all of these, with the exception of the one addressed to Judah,[1] were originally spoken by Amos himself before an Israelitic crowd gathered in the temple court at Bethel for the new year festivals, just one year before his banishment.

Now back to Amos' sermon. The opening *word* is at once the introduction to the book and to his sermon. It may have been a kind of motto used many times as a means of getting the attention of the crowd before beginning his real message.

> It is Yahweh from Zion who roars,
>   and from Jerusalem whose voice sounds out
> that the pastures of the shepherds shall mourn
>   and the top of Carmel shall wither.

Such a cry should certainly serve effectively in getting attention. But it also serves as a key to the message of Amos. He is a Judean, a consecrated servant of Yahweh. He knows the proper place of Yahweh worship to be in Jerusalem. This does not mean that he thinks of God as being bound to a particular place. Yahweh certainly speaks to him and guides him in his work in Israel. Nor does it mean that Yahweh is not the God of Israel. Quite the contrary.

Amos proclaims God's claim to the full allegiance and worship of all Israel. But this statement stands out in sharp opposition to Israel's habits of worship in Bethel and the other sanctuaries of the Northern Kingdom. Yahweh is not the God of Bethel, Gilgal, or even Beer-sheba. He is not to be sought in the cult of these

---

[1] I follow the majority of modern exegetes in viewing the prophecy against Judah as a later addition. This addition is in the form of an application of Amos' very message and spirit to the later age which treasured and appreciated it. It is essentially the sharp difference in the accusations against Judah, expressed in a style and a mode of thinking which are so typical of the era of the Deuteronomist, which leads to this conclusion.

sanctuaries. He may be found in obedience, in repentance, in prayer anywhere, but he has specifically associated himself with Zion and Jerusalem and with no other place.

Further, the message of Zion's God for the people of Israel is one of judgment and destruction. In these two short statements the message of Amos is accurately comprehended.

On the heels of this introduction follow seven *messages*, styled in the manner of a runner who delivers his message orally. He begins, "Thus says so and so, ' Thus and thus and thus,' " and closes with a repetition of the name of the sender. Somewhere, also, in such a message the name of the receiver should appear. This is the form which Amos uses as he presents orally God's messages, word by word, to the people.

Amos further uses a fixed introductory formula to introduce each of the seven messages: "For three transgressions of _____, and [even] for four, I will not revoke the punishment [turn it back]." The words are remarkable for their pungent, arresting style on the one hand and for their deliberate vagueness on the other.

One transgression (rebellion) is worthy of the death penalty. Evidently the numbers three and four are used symbolically to indicate the fulness, the completion of the sin. But these three transgressions are never listed as such; only an example is given in each instance. The reference remains vague throughout, deliberately so.

This vagueness comes out even more clearly in the reference to "it" in the last clause. "I shall not revoke it." What is this *it?* The reference must be to judgment of some kind which has been fixed. It is most likely that it suggests the coming day of Yahweh and its related judgment. The popular eschatology of Israel understood that great day to include judgment upon the nations.

Amos consistently proclaimed that the judgment would be upon Israel as well.

See him as he ascends an elevated projection of the temple

court. His boorish clothing and appearance, his commanding
countenance, his piercing eyes, and above all his repeated shout-
ing of the introductory motto have attracted a considerable group
gathered for a great feast day. The festive crowd subsides into
hushed, expectant silence below him. His harsh Judean Hebrew
rings out clearly across the temple court:

Thus says Yahweh:
"For three transgressions of Damascus
   and for four, I will not revoke it;
because they have threshed Gilead with iron points,
I shall send fire into the house of Hazael,
   and it shall devour the citadels of Ben-hadad.
And I shall break in pieces the bar of Damascus
   and cut off the inhabitant from the Valley of Aven,
and the one holding the scepter from Beth-eden;
   and the people of Aram [Syria] shall go into exile to Kir,"
                                              says Jahweh.

This pronouncement of punishment on a national enemy meets
with instant approval, evidenced by a shout which gradually
quiets to a murmur of approval. Above the murmur the "thus
says the Lord" of the prophet begins the second message.

"Now this is preaching!" the crowd whispers. "This is prophecy
as it ought to be. It looks like that wild Judean has come to his
senses after all." The expectant crowd eagerly welcomes the
proclamation of the near day of Jahweh, when God would finally
prove his lordship over all the nations by raising Israel to its
destined place of favor and distinction.

The crowd responds to each name of another enemy nation
with growing fervor. Philistia, then Tyre, Edom, Ammon, and
Moab are each greeted with a shout, which gives positive proof
of the partisan sympathy of the crowd.

As the prophet begins the intonation of the now familiar
formula for the climactic seventh time, the people are already
thinking ahead of him—"This time perhaps Egypt—or even bet-

ter Assyria." As the prophet builds up to the name of the seventh object of Yahweh's judgment, the crowd prepares for the response to which it has been conditioned. Perhaps they even begin to shout before the significance of the name pierced home: "*Israel!* For three transgressions of *Israel.*" Had they heard aright?

The shocked silence of the crowd makes the words of Amos ring clearly, unforgettably across the court: "Because they sold a righteous [the righteous] one for silver and the poor for a pair of shoes."

The prophet is on a familiar theme before an audience made defenseless by the preparatory messages. Israel will not escape the judgment of the day of Yahweh. Judgment is sure and devastating upon the corrupt society and the bribed courts of the land. Amos follows up his initial advantage with a devastating indictment:

> Those lusting after the dust of the earth at the
>   expense of the poor,
>   who pervert the way (of justice) of the humble,
> while a man and his father go to the same girl
>   in order to profane my holy name.

Lust and cupidity have robbed the nation of its heritage of sensitivity to justice and right. The worship at the illicit sanctuaries with their corrupting influences of Canaanite worship has taken its toll among the people. Elijah's victories over the Tyrian Baal had been emptied of real significance by the adoption of domestic Canaanite theology and practice in the local sanctuaries under the name of Yahweh worship. Now Amos is spelling out the real consequences for the people.

Yahweh's message traces the work of election and redemption which he had performed for them but which had gone for naught. They have thought of their prosperity and strength as something they themselves gained; if not directly, then through the literal fulfilment of cultic requirements. Consistently they have denied the chosen spokesman of God a chance to present God's message. All of this has brought about a national weakness, a religious senility, a moral depravity of which the Israelites seem utterly unaware. The message that Amos brings spells out in detail their utter defeat.

This is the impression that the sermon must have made upon its audience that memorable day in Bethel. But the sermon has a great deal more to say to us.

The prophecies against the nations are significant. The fact that they appear in the work of the earliest writing prophet indicates that "foreign prophecies" are an integral part of classical prophecy in Israel. In Amos the function of these prophecies is not, like the exilic prophets, that of clearing the way for the return of Israel to her own land.

The judgments are not so much teleological here as they are true judgments—punitive judgments on a moral basis. They serve to emphasize the proclamation of God's sovereignty over all nations. Yahweh's rule and power is not limited to Israel alone, and these judgments will fall upon them, not through defeat before Israel but through direct decree and action of God.

God's moral claims apply to all. But there is also a common thread running through them which should not be overlooked.

Assyria was the big power of that day. For almost a century she had been occupied with internal problems which had prevented her assertion of strength in the west. Had the little states of Palestine and Syria been able to muster leadership which could see beyond their petty differences, they could have formed an alliance capable of holding Assyrian forces at a distance, as they had done at the battle of Qarqar. But the little states had wasted their time, strength, and life quarreling among themselves. This is clearly presented by Amos in the indictments upon the first six nations.

Ignoring the signs that the colossus of the north was stirring to new life, Palestine and Syria remained divided and continued to quarrel. Amos sees this as both sin and judgment. These nations stood within the boundaries of the promised Davidic kingdom. Adequate vision and leadership of a messianic character might well have brought the unity and influence of a second Davidic era, as indeed such circumstances plus such leadership did bring for a very short time under Josiah a century later.

Amos' indictment is not only moral and religious but it carries a note of political insight into a chance now lost which should not be missed. Amos must take his place alongside his distinguished successors as a keen assessor of the political situation.

Although his indictment of Israel runs along a different line, we can detect an awareness of the moral weakness of the nation. This excludes any thought that one could expect from her the kind of strength and leadership which could accomplish the dream of unifying these little powers. Nothing is left for her but defeat—a defeat which is a judgment upon her faithlessness toward God.

This internal degeneration had clearest expression in social life. The Canaanite emphasis on material things had displaced the Israelite emphasis on man as the main value under God. So, rich and enterprising men crushed both men and justice in their greed for wealth and luxury.

Amos is in the direct line of Elijah in putting his great emphasis on this element of Israel's sin. This is indeed the clearest sign that Israel had abandoned the law of God.

All of life, to Amos, presents itself as a unity. Morality and religion are intimately associated with society and politics. It is not even possible to describe this in "cause-and-effect" relations. It is much more intimately related than that. It is part of a realm of being for Israel, in history and under God.

3

Tested by a Plumb Line

The Third Period (7:7-17; 3-6)

Tested by a plumb line (7:7-9).—The third vision shows a wall under construction. The Lord himself is testing the vertical angle with a plumb line. "The Lord said to me, 'Amos, what do you see?' and I said, 'a plumb line.' Then the Lord said, 'Behold, I am setting a plumb line in the midst of my people Israel; I will never again pass by them.'"

The meaning of this vision differs from the previous ones in two important respects: First, it indicates a judgment which falls with careful discrimination upon those who do not measure (fulfil) up to God's standards (requirements); second, it has a note of finality which is lacking in the first two visions.

The symbol of the plumb line is remarkably apt in showing that God will apply his standard to his people in order to determine the relative guilt among them. What this standard is exactly is not here stated. But we do not have to seek far in the "words" of Amos to know. It is the standard of justice and righteousness which God has given to his people and which he expects them to fulfil. It is his law, the expression of his will within the covenant which so many in Israel were treating with flagrant disregard.

Against the threat of this kind of judgment it is impossible to raise the plea that it is "unfair" or "unwarranted," for it assumes a careful weighing of guilt before the sentence falls. For this reason this judgment can be final and irrevocable in a sense in which the others were not.

Through these three visions one can trace a development in the doctrine of judgment which is instructive. The first concept of judgment as chastisement which should lead the people to righteousness did show that God had a positive purpose in judgment, but as a complete doctrine it proved inadequate. The second concept of the overflowing and all-consuming wrath of God did justice to his great and awesome being but proved arbitrary and ill-adapted to express Amos' high concept of God's character and will. Both of these may be applied in part, but neither may be used alone.

This third vision is more final than the first. There is no question here of simply chastising, or of simply luring the people to repentance. It is also more individual and specific in its application than the second, with its apparent concept of community guilt and total destruction.

Amos is led here to see judgment as applied according to a standard. Guilt which incurs judgment comes from a deliberate flaunting of the expressed will of God. God will measure that guilt and apply his judgment. This does not imply that the idea of the day of Yahweh has been rejected but that it is now being defined. The second period had emphasized that Israel, too, would feel the effect of punishment on the day of God's intervention. It is in this third period that this judgment is focused more exactly. This focus comes to rest, with much heavier accents than before, on the sanctuaries and finally on the royal house.

It is also to be noted that this teaching concerning judgment leaves room for God to work out his will through the people who remain when the infectious sin of the ruling house and the sanctuaries is removed.

Messages stressing this type of judgment on the monarchy and the sanctuaries may be traced in chapters 3-6. They are here related to this third period of Amos' ministry.

Election and judgment (3:1-2).—Surely the objection against this preaching of Amos which found immediate expression among the people was that it contradicted the promises of God. Through God's deliverance from Egypt and his subsequent covenant with them, he had permanently undertaken to be their God. It was unthinkable for them that this election could mean anything else than God's continued unconditioned blessing and salvation. Their position is strong insofar as it is based on actual Yahwistic theology.

But Amos immediately brands their understanding as partial, and, therefore, false. Election implies responsibility as well as privilege.

Hear this word that the Lord has spoken against you, O people of Israel, against the whole family which I brought up out of the land of Egypt: "You only have I known of all the families of the earth; therefore, I will punish you for all your iniquities."

Amos is using "Israel" here in its religious sense, as the elect people of God. He points out that this election is unique and applies to no other people as it does to Israel. But the judgment which is so proclaimed is only conceivable within the framework of such election.

Election, as known in Israel, exists within a framework of covenant. If it may be argued that the original salvation from Egypt was basically unconditioned, it must certainly be recognized that this expression of God's free grace is completed by a covenant with the people which is strictly conditioned.

Within this framework of covenant election, salvation is conditioned upon the people's response in faith and obedience to the revelation of God's will in his law. But the possibility of judgment in the event of infidelity or disobedience is present within

the covenant from the beginning. It is this which Amos emphasizes in complete agreement with the Mosaic legislation.

It is also pertinent to point out that here, too, Amos insists on
the continued free sovereignty of God. Within the realm of election he is still sovereign. His will is supreme.

A further observation is in order. Note the emphasis on the
personal pronouns "you" and "I." Relation to God is a personal
one for Amos. Every aspect of his faith is personal, as the visionary experiences so clearly show. Therefore, his concepts of
sovereignty and of election are also personal.

This passage continues to have a pertinent message to us
today. Our recognition of God's rule over our lives and our relation to him should be even more absolute in Christ, who is Lord
of all, than Amos could possibly have experienced it. We, too,
must learn that both judgment and salvation are to be understood only within realms fixed by God's covenant grace in Jesus
Christ.

The principle of moral causality (3:3-4,8).—"Do two
walk together, unless they have agreed? Does a lion roar in the
forest when he has no prey? The lion has roared; who will not
fear? The Lord God has spoken; who can but prophesy?"

The prophet's message here turns on two things which are
closely related. The first has to do with the very fact of his
prophecy. When people asked, "Why are you bothering us here
in this way?" the answer to Amos was obvious.

"There is a basic reason for my prophecy and it is none other
than God himself. God has spoken to me. I can do nothing else
than prophesy."

The second question has to do with the content of his message
and touches on a fundamental tenet of Amos' theology. He believed firmly in the principle of *moral causality.* What people
are will inevitably show itself in their lives. This is not so because of some natural tendency but because Yahweh is the Lord.
His will is moral, and he has decreed that "whatsoever a man

sows, that shall he also reap." When judgment comes upon the people, it is the Lord's doing and comes because of their sin.

Israel's judgment (3:9-11).—The message which follows is a direct application of the principle just mentioned. These two messages could have formed a part of the same speech.

Amos points his accusing finger at the discontent, the eruptions of violence in the land, and the oppressions of the poor, and says that they are caused by the moral degeneracy of the people. Such disorder and weakness inevitably follow disobedience to God's moral law.

The people have sinned so deeply that "they do not know how to do right." They are evidently unaware that injustice and immorality simply serve to "store up violence and robbery in their fortresses." But God knows and Israel's great enemies know.

Amos summons the great world powers of the day to observe the internal weakness and corruption in Samaria. As they draw their conclusions, they will prepare to add Israel again to the list of tributary vassals. Because of this internal moral weakness, the judgment of God is obvious. The enemy will indeed come, destroy, and subdue.

An objection answered (3:12).—Someone in the crowd must have shouted an objection—"But surely Yahweh would not allow that! Surely he would rescue his people from such a fate!"

Amos' answer is couched in bitter irony: "Thus says the Lord: 'As the shepherd rescues from the mouth of the lion two legs, or a piece of an ear, so shall the people of Israel who dwell in Samaria be rescued, with the corner of a couch or . . . a bed.'"

It is to be observed that when a shepherd lost a sheep given to his charge, he was required by ancient law to account for it. If it was lost to a wild animal, a part of a leg bone or a piece of an ear served as evidence of its destruction. This served to allay suspicion that the shepherd may have sold it for his own gain. But such is not a "rescue" at all. Quite the contrary—it is evidence of destruction.

So Amos says, "The only rescue which Israel will have will be like that." This is not a teaching of a remnant (although that may be found elsewhere in Amos) but a rejection of the unfounded assurance which some people held that God would be "too good" to allow them to experience full judgment for their sins.

Errors in religion (3:13-15).—"Hear, and testify against the house of Jacob . . . that on the day I punish Israel for his transgressions, I will punish the altars of Bethel." This prophecy makes specific one aspect of the general judgment against Israel.

Bethel was one of the two places chosen by Jeroboam I as a national sanctuary. It was particularly related to the crown and to the very separate existence of the Northern Kingdom. Here the symbol of the golden calf ruled. By its very existence as a national and royal sanctuary it stood for religion (and, therefore, for God) as the servant of state policy and well-being. For this very reason we may suppose that it felt the inroads of Canaanite ways of thinking more than some other Yahwistic sanctuaries had done. It is no wonder that Amos picks it from all the rest as the focus for his prophecies of destruction.

It is interesting to note here also how this judgment on the sanctuary is joined to a judgment on the houses of the rich. Religion and economic exploitation went hand in hand in Israel. Amos never tires of mocking these strange companions and of pronouncing God's judgment equally on both.

The Bible has a great deal to say about economics. The pertinence of Yahweh's will, as well as that of Christ, to this area of life cannot be doubted by one who reads his Bible with open eyes. The message is basically one. All things belong to God. He who recognizes God as the Lord will use "things" and wealth according to the will of God and for the glory of God. This will of God certainly includes, as a minimum, justice to all men and, as a maximum, love toward all men. It is interesting that the Bible has much more to say about justice and right for the worker than about the rights of property. But this aspect of biblical teaching has seldom received proper attention. All too often, as in Amos' day, official religion has supported the exploitation of the poor. When this is true, every true man of God will react as Amos did by denouncing it as a sham and as utterly false to the God it professes.

Women in Samaria (4:1-3).—This prophecy also belongs to the critical ministry of Amos. Here the simple Judean herdsman addresses his words to the fine ladies of the capital whose insatiable thirst for wealth and luxury knew no limits imposed by justice or honesty. Their greed merely spurred the ambition and lust of their husbands to greater lengths.

With bitter sarcasm, Amos cries: "Hear this word, you cows of Bashan, who are in the mountain of Samaria." Bashan produced fine, prized cattle, and Amos' use of this figure to describe the fat, spoiled women of the rich must have drawn a chuckle from his male hearers. But his intention is dead serious. He is announcing an end to the way of life which has supported them. Captivity by their enemies will make them to be led out of their "stalls" to be taken far away, prodded on by a herdsman's hooks. In those brutal days this last had a literal meaning in the handling of prisoners which reflects barbarous and merciless treatment. Judgment upon Samaria and all her ways is about to begin for Israel, because of her continued sin and rebellion against her rightful Lord and God.

Come to Bethel, and transgress (4:4-5).—Offering sacrifices and performing religious observances at Bethel are in themselves rebellious acts against the true God, according to Amos' cry. Here is bitter sarcasm. These are the things that the people "love to do." They do them to satisfy their own wishes, not to please God. This is natural religion. This is the "religion" which everyone feels in his heart he needs and which causes men everywhere to worship something. It is the religious urge which is so easily satisfied with ritual and its trappings.

This is the kind of thing which Jesus criticized so heavily in the Jews of his day, which Paul called "a zeal . . . but not according to knowledge" (Rom. 10:2, KJV). This kind of "religion" pacifies the conscience and temporarily relieves the "urge to religion" in the human heart. It never transforms life. It never brings moral renewal. It is corrupt and rotten from the beginning.

In a day when this "urge to religion" is being expressed in people in many parts of our Western world, it is vitally necessary that we be able to distinguish with prophetic insight the difference between true religion and false. For one is of the flesh human, whereas the one which is true is of the spirit, spiritual and divine. One soothes the human spirit; the other brings on the crisis which leads to repentance. One kind adapts itself to the life and ways of the worshiper. The true kind transforms the worshiper into the image of his Lord.

Our faith is not basically an ethic any more than was Amos' faith. But the fact that God's will is fundamentally moral and spiritual puts the ethical issues at the center of the life given to his follower. In the true worshiper one may legitimately expect a moral and spiritual renewal, reorientation, and revival. When there is no sign of this, one may rightly ask whether the faith we proclaim is the true message and power of God.

Previous judgments but no repentance (4:6-12).—This passage has already been mentioned as a record of an earlier phase of Amos' ministry. Judgments of famine, drought, crop failure (including locusts), pestilence, and earthquake are listed. We should probably assume that each of these in turn had been interpreted by a prophet, Amos or some other, as God's judgment, along with the plea for the people to repent and turn to God.

Yet, after each account stands the pathetic statement, "Yet you did not return to me." We may also think of the warnings of both Isaiah and Jeremiah. Although they preached, the people would not listen. In each case was the sincere intention of converting the people to faith and repentance (cf. Ezek. 18). Even when the people do not listen (cf. Ezek. 33:7-9), it is also clear that such preaching and such judgment fulfils a certain function. In case they do not heed the warning, prophetic preaching prepares the way for and justifies judgment against them. Such has been the case with the judgments here referred to.

"Therefore thus will I do to you, O Israel; . . . prepare to meet your God, O Israel!"

The time of chastisement and warning is past. The people have fixed their own sentence. Their judgment is about to be pronounced.

Hymn to Yahweh (4:12-13; 5:6-9; 9:5-6).—As Amos calls Israel to prepare to meet her judge, he breaks into a quotation from an old hymn to Yahweh which must have been known to the people. The hymn stresses the majestic and awful character of Yahweh as Creator, judge, and condescending ruler. Fragments of such a hymn are found in three places in Amos, but these three themes are not grouped together in these fragmentary quotations. Yet it seems right to view them all as coming from the same hymn. A possible reconstruction of the way the old hymn may have been sung is as follows:

The first strophe is found in Amos 4:12-13:

> Prepare to meet your God, O Israel!
> Former of mountains,
>   Creator of wind,
>   One revealing to man what His thought is,
> Making dawn of darkness,
>   And treading upon the heights of the earth
> Is He whose name is Yahweh, God of hosts.

The second strophe is found in Amos 5:6-9:

> Seek Yahweh and live!
>   Lest He break out like fire
>   Which consumes beyond quenching.
> Yahweh (it is who) caused justice to trickle down from above

And established righteousness for the earth,[1]
Making Pleiades and Orion
  Turning deep darkness to morning,
    Who darkened day into night.
The One causing Taurus to vanquish Capella
  And who will cause Taurus to set upon Vindemiatrix
    Is He whose name is Yahweh.[2]

The third strophe is found in chapter 9, verses 5-6:

Lord Yahweh
  The One summoning signs
    Is the One touching the earth so it will quiver,
Though all its inhabitants mourn with it
  And its reservoirs rise like the Nile
    And irrigate like the Nile of Egypt.
One determining his thoughts (works) in the heavens is He,
  His bounty which he will establish on the earth.
The One calling to the sea's water
  That he might pour it over the earth's surface
    Is He whose name is Yahweh.

Amos appears here to have turned back to this hymn again and again to stress, through its emphasis on God's power in creation and control over nature, that he is truly God of all. Such a great and powerful God is the one before whom now Israel must stand for judgment.

    Lament over Israel (5:1-9,16-17).—The singing of such a lament is a fairly common device of the prophets. It stresses the certainty of the coming judgment by treating it as an accomplished fact. The lament is particularly effective in that it pictures Israel as having failed to fulfil her destiny, like a young virgin who dies without having married and borne children.

    The terrible destruction which will befall her is pictured. But

---

[1]An explanation of this reading is given in "Note on the Text of Amos V, 7," *Vetus Testimentum* IV (1954), 215.
[2]See *Vision and Prophecy in Amos* (Grand Rapids: Wm. B. Eerdman's Publishing Co., 1958), pp. 55 f.

the pronouncement of judgment is broken by a moving plea to the people: "Thus says the Lord to the house of Israel: 'seek me and live; but do not seek Bethel, and do not enter into Gilgal or cross over to Beer-sheba; for Gilgal shall surely go into exile, and Bethel shall come to nought.'"

In these verses we can see the application of the principle given in the third vision. The plumb line standard shows that the focus of judgment is to be upon the false sanctuaries. To go to them is not "to seek Yahweh." He must be sought directly. They and all that they stand for must be utterly destroyed.

And then a line of the hymn, which is so similar to the prophetic cry just given, prompts the prophet (or the compiler of his prophecies) to quote the familiar hymn. The one they must seek as Saviour is, indeed, the Creator and the judge of all the earth.

Does one find God when he comes to our churches, listens to our sermons, and hears our public prayers? It is a disturbing thought that sometimes God has had to say: "Do not go to the churches or to the preachers, for you will not find me there." May it be that this judgment will never have to be placed on us! But if it may be true at some time or in some place, be assured that God will not allow himself to be cut off from people who want to find him. "They who seek shall find!"

"In all the squares there shall be wailing . . . for I will pass through the midst of you" (vv. 16-17). This continues the kind of judgment decreed in the lament above. It is interesting to note that judgment here is brought about by Yahweh's presence in passing through them, as on the day of Egypt's affliction in the death of her firstborn.

God's presence may be the occasion of salvation, the symbol of his greatest blessing. But it may also be the occasion of judgment (cf. the pertinent passages in Ex. 32 f.). How can this be? It is so because God is holy. Those who can "abide the day of his coming" must be holy or fulfil the conditions of holiness. For the power of this holiness may be positive in granting blessing or devastatingly negative in judging that one who is not holy.

It is important that we notice that the people who will be smitten by this holy presence are those who have fulfilled all the rites of holiness at the sanctuary. These rites do not prepare them for the presence of God. The sanctified, according to Bethel's ways, will be the judged and destroyed ones. Amos understands that moral transgressions may not simply be wiped clean through a ritual. This holiness of God is sensitive to moral sin and reacts negatively to it particularly.

Luxury and corruption (5:10-15).—The rich who have made their fortunes through the exploitation of the poor are described in eloquent terms. "They hate him who reproves in the gate, and they abhor him who speaks the truth." The reference to the gate is to the common meeting place of the people where cases of justice are tried before an assembled jury of men. This had been the time-honored spot where any man could receive justice when his case was heard by the men of the town.

The exploiting rich carried a personal grudge against any man who dared to speak out against them in the court as their judge, or who dare testify as a witness to their deeds.

But God's condemnation fell on the men who should act as judges. This use of the power of the rich had corrupted those who had always been charged with the maintenance of justice in Israel, the free men themselves. They had lost their integrity as free and honest men. In its place they had wealth in houses and vineyards. But judgment for their deeds would not allow them to enjoy their ill-gotten gain. Yahweh is the one who upholds justice and who demands it from all men. How great his judgment would be against those who "afflict the righteous [one]" instead of judging in his favor, "who take a bribe and turn aside the needy in the gate!" For judgment in Israel was no longer on the merits of the case, and only the rich could gain a hearing.

The system of judgment here presupposed is a very old and

very democratic one. Only at a very late date was there any such thing as a state code of law in Israel. Most cases of law were handled by a gathering of a group of the town citizens "in the gate." For centuries the system had functioned well. There was no distinction between persons, and any citizen, no matter how poor or lowly, could get justice by calling together the men in this way. Each man felt a personal responsibility for the maintenance of justice and order.

Long centuries of depending on the rulers to provide both order and justice has robbed the modern world of much of this conception of a personal responsibility for justice and order. But modern democracy has put back into the hands of ordinary men the power and responsibility for establishing and maintaining good government.

Some of those who were condemned by Amos were actually guilty of crimes. But it was not necessary for most of them to actually do something wrong. They had only to be silent and not disturb the machinations of the real evildoers. They received their bribe for simply remaining dumb and blind to the evil around them. So Amos rightly notes that they were parties to the crime and had to bear their guilt as well. Failure to assume and properly carry out the responsibilities which a democratic state places upon its citizens leaves them open to the same charge which Amos leveled against men of his day.

With such men Amos pleads: "Seek good, and not evil, that you may live: and so the Lord, the God of hosts, will be with you, as you have said. Hate evil, and love good, and establish justice in the gate; it may be that the Lord, the God of hosts, will be gracious to the remnant of Joseph."

What Amos requires here is a change in their way of life, a reestablishment in them of right standards of thinking and of living. This was the sign of genuine repentance which might even yet turn back Yahweh's wrath enough for some of them to be saved.

One word which demands attention is Amos' reference to a "remnant." It is commonplace to assume that Isaiah first taught a doctrine of a remnant. It is clear that Isaiah is the man principally responsible for the formulation of the doctrine as known in Judah. But our increased knowledge of Canaanite cult ceremonies points to an origin of the idea in the ritual drama rather than in history.

Semitic ritual generally featured a sham battle between the forces of good and evil. This drama ended with bodies piled high and only a very small group of the original army remained. This group became the original "remnant." For Israel, this was not a battle between divine forces. It was God's judgment on the world. But the result follows the dramatic pattern, with many destroyed and few left—the remnant. It is increasingly clear that many eschatological features of Israelitic prophecy are drawn from this drama. This then is applied historically.

We should not be surprised that Amos based his hope beyond the judgment on such a remnant, just as Isaiah and others would do later. The doctrine of the remnant in Israel was already firmly fixed. Amos did not challenge the basic idea.

In chapters 1-2, as he pictured the judgment upon the nations, it seems evident that Amos intended to dispute the popular belief that Israel as a whole was the blessed remnant. He rather identified it as a "remnant of Joseph," later even as a remnant of a remnant, and specifically as that part which should prove capable of repentance and renewal.

The day of the Lord (5:18-20).—"Woe to you who desire the day of the Lord! Why would you have the day of the Lord? It is darkness, and not light."

Ordinary Israelites eagerly awaited the coming of the great day. Perhaps they thought about it in terms like those of ancient festivals in which the dawn of a bright and clear New Year's Day was awaited as an omen of good luck throughout the year to follow. For this reason many ancient temples were so built facing the east that the first rays of the rising sun would fall upon the altar. So the Israelites expected the great day of Yahweh to be a day of dawning good fortune for them.

Amos denies this. For them the day of Yahweh would be a day of darkest judgment because of their sin and corruption, a day in which judgment would follow judgment, and none would escape. In this we see Amos' understanding of moral sovereignty assuming a dominant position in his eschatology as well. It is exactly in such matters that Canaanite and Yahwistic theology are poles apart. The Canaanite could understand a doctrine of free grace or one of undeserved election in terms of fate which was not to be questioned. He could never understand the stern requirements of Israel's moral law nor the idea of God's moral righteousness which was incorruptible and unchangeable, even by a bribe of offerings and sacrifices.

Not worship but life (5:21-27).—"I hate, I despise your feasts, and I take no delight in your solemn assemblies." The trappings and forms of formal worship are here categorically rejected. The Israelites assumed that to please God they must simply perform outward religious duties of sacrifice and worship. If they paid their tithes and observed the sabbath, God would certainly bless them. Amos' message must have come as quite a shock to them.

Their offerings and songs were insulting and annoying rather than pleasing to God. What does this mean? Is formal worship with its sacrifice, public prayer, and other worship forms actually contrary to the will of God?

Amos positively states: "Let justice roll down like waters, and righteousness like an everflowing stream." This should not be taken to mean that one must simply substitute ethical ordinances for ritual requirements. Jesus had to take his stand against legalism of this kind for the same reason that Amos did. True religion is to be a thing of the inner life and of the spirit, not an outer, formal thing. It should be a transforming, renewing experience for the whole man. It is not enough for one to dress up and go to church on Sunday. True worship consists in living according to the will and power of God in justice and in righteousness.

The following verse raises the question concerning the historical origin of sacrifice. There can be little doubt that the Israelites in the wilderness practiced some kinds of sacrifice. But Amos is reflecting good historical sense in noting that the principal sacrificial forms used in his day were of Canaanite origin. In some instances they had been adapted to a Yahwistic service in an admirable way, as many of our extant regulations for sacrifice in the Pentateuch will show. But in much of their usage in the sanctuaries of northern Israel they still had heathen connotations. They were still temptations which led the people to worship foreign gods. For this reason, Amos indicates, the people must go into exile.

The prophetic criticism of sacrifice (of which Amos is typical) insists that such outer worship is simply a means—a shell. When this shell is filled with true faith and obedience on the part of the worshipers, it may have value and usefulness. When, as in Amos' day, people use this shell as a substitute for living faith and obedience, it is empty and worse than nothing—an insult to God and the worst kind of sin. In the midst of the current revival of liturgy which is being felt everywhere, this should be a constant warning to us today as well.

So long as it is an instrument of and a means toward new life and a real meeting with God, so long as it leads the worshipers to do the will of God, ritual and form may be both legitimate and good. As soon as the satisfying experience of such worship takes the place of a real meeting with God, a true response to his demand for repentance and faith, and a compulsion to obedience toward our Lord, it must be branded as a mockery and a falsehood, even as Amos branded it.

The sin of indifference (6:1-7).—"Woe to those who depend without a care on Zion, and to those who are trusting in the mountain of Samaria." Amos' cry is the second of his three woes. It is directed against those whose self-assurance has robbed them of their ordinary powers of judgment and concern. They are the princes of the people, proud of their military power, and willing to risk it needlessly. They judge their military powers by their success against their neighbors. They are urged to take a more realistic view of the situation in which Assyria is the main threat, not to continue the kind of continual raiding with the little states which Amos had condemned in chapters 1 and 2. These are the men whose refusal to face up to the seriousness of the Assyrian threat merely meant that the day of violence for the whole land was drawing nearer.

"Woe to those who lie upon beds of ivory . . . but are not grieved over the ruin of Joseph." This third woe is spoken against those basking in luxury with careless indifference to the inner ruin and the outer danger of their people. History so often repeats this picture of the luxurious rich reveling on, even as judgment knocks upon their doors, through rioting mobs or invading vandals.

These triple woes have struck at those whose security and indifference are based on their false religious trust, those whose arrogant pride is based on a false trust in military strength, those whose languid ease exists because their eyes are shut to the needs and dangers around them. These will lead the procession of prisoners on the way to exile on that day of judgment.

The sin of selfish indifference continues to plague mankind. There are still religions which are nothing more than "opiates," soothing a people into blissful indifference to the signs of corruption and human need about them. There are still those pompous parade-ground generals who with no sense of responsibility would plunge into hopeless and useless carnage. There are still those around us who sip their drinks of luxury in careless ease with no thought for the staggering problems of their peoples or the desperate needs of their neighbors. When these become typical of any society, that society is also ripe for judgment and destruction. Western society is often termed degenerate by its enemies. We may do well to apply to ourselves the standards of judgment which Amos used and ask if this judgment is also due our civilization.

The blindness of sin (6:11-14).—"Do horses run upon rocks? Does one plow the sea with oxen? But you have turned justice into poison and the fruit of righteousness into wormwood."

Amos begins by announcing that Yahweh has already commanded the coming judgment. Then he asks these two questions. The answer to each of them would be, "Of course not!" It would seem just as obvious to any intelligent person that the strength of a nation can be maintained only at its own heart through justice and right.

When corruptions had swept the courts and the sturdy class of landowning farmers who had always formed the backbone of Israelite society had been reduced through economic suppression to a group of groveling peasants, they no longer were capable of defending their country. But the dull aristocratic rich took no account of this when they declared that their country was invincible.

For the logical mind of the prophet this inner corruption could not fail to be matched by a fall. He announces that God is already raising up a nation to fulfil his judgment by oppressing Israel throughout the length of her land. Already the reviving power of Assyria is drawing into the prophet's field of vision. His principle of moral causality already points to the disastrous results which an Assyrian campaign through the West would bring at this time.

Judgment on sanctuary and palace (7:9).—The messages which we have surveyed in chapters 4-6 illustrate the increasingly direct attack of the prophet on Bethel and Samaria, on the sanctuary and the royal house. Through the first two periods the central features of the prophet's message had not differed essentially from those of any prophet of God. True he had indicted Israel for her sin. But it was still within the bounds of loyalty expected of a prophet.

But by the time Amos approached Bethel for the great New Year's Day festival in 750 B.C. with the hordes of pilgrims from all parts of Israel, his message had become definite: "The high places of Isaac shall be made desolate, and the sanctuaries of Israel shall be laid waste, and I will rise against the house of Jeroboam with the sword."

This was no general prophecy against the people. The standard of God's judgment had been applied to Israel, and the guilt of the royal sanctuaries and the royal house had been indicated. The story which follows clearly shows the implications and results of this prophecy.

Amos in Bethel (7:10-17).—The announcement of this prophecy in Bethel must have brought to the mind of Amaziah, the priest, memories of earlier prophetic revolts such as had brought even the currently reigning house of Jehu to power. This prophecy sounded like treason and a call to revolt. He immediately reported the event to his sovereign.

But, without waiting for a reply from Samaria, he acted to try to get the troublesome Amos away from the great crowd gathered at Bethel. The crowd could easily become inflamed by a revolutionary preacher and break into real violence. So, he tried to deal with Amos personally: "O seer, go, flee away to the land of Judah, and eat bread there, and prophesy there; but never again prophesy at Bethel, for it is the king's sanctuary, and it is a temple of the kingdom."

He seemed to be accustomed to dealing with prophets around the temple who earned their bread by their prophecies. A threat like this would have sent any one of them flying. It is clear that Amaziah had recognized Amos as a Judean, perhaps through his rough herdsman's cloak or by his southern accent. His recognition of the nature of the message may have led him to believe that Amos was a hired agitator sent into the country from Judah.

His statement concerning the sanctuary revealed the true state of affairs in Bethel. It was not the temple of Yahweh, the Most High. He said, "It is a royal chapel." The important thing about this church is that the king worships here. It is established and maintained for the welfare and well-being of the kingdom. No such treacherous words as you have spoken are allowed here.

The roughly dressed countryman from Tekoah must have drawn himself to his full height to look at this priest with scornful eyes, as he answered: "I am no prophet, nor a prophet's son; but I am a herdsman, and a dresser of sycamore trees" (v. 14, RSV). Perhaps Amaziah had not seen a man like this in Israel. The independent breed of men who counted all men their equal and bowed before no one had almost been extinguished in the Northern Kingdom. In the rough desert country of Judah such men still lived who had never beheld a creature before whom they felt inferiority or fear. Such a man was Amos, and he begins by making it quite clear that he does not belong to the subservient prophet class who earn their bread around the sanctuaries by fulfilling the requirements of the arrogant worshipers and priests.

"The Lord took me from following the flock, and the Lord said to me, 'Go, prophesy to my people Israel.'" In this sentence the emphasis is on *the Lord* in contrast to Amaziah's emphasis on *the royalty* of Bethel. If Amaziah derived his authority from the king, Amos makes it quite clear that his authority and his mandate came directly from God. Some of the noblest moments in the history of prophecy have been when a man of God resolutely stated his divine authority in the face of royal pressure. Such men were Nathan, Micah, Elijah, and now Amos. These noble men worked under a divine commission which overshadowed any royal decree. They could not be cowed by a show of force or blustering authority.

Amos turned upon Amaziah the full force of God's anger

against those who oppose him. Amaziah had dared try to silence God's appointed messenger. Now a special judgment was to fall upon him and all that were his. And God's judgment on Israel was more imminent than ever: "Israel shall surely go into exile away from the land."

There the account ends. But the implication is that Amos *did* have to leave Israel. He must have returned reluctantly to his home or to some sanctuary in Judah, disappointed that he could not remain to see the fulfilment of his promises, perhaps with a broken heart that his pleadings had brought so few to repentance before the coming wrath.

This dramatic episode at Bethel marked the end of Amos' ministry *in* Israel. But it certainly did not mark the end of his prophecy *concerning* the people of Israel. The continuation of his prophetic ministry is recorded in the two final chapters of his book. His prophecies continued to be directed toward the Northern Kingdom, even as he worked from exile in his home country. They ring with his unshaken faith that the word of God will certainly be fulfilled and confirmed by God's own action.

4

A Basket of Summer Fruit

The Fourth Period (8:1-14)

The end (vv. 1-3).—The fourth vision presents an object to which Amos' attention is particularly drawn. It was a common, everyday thing. A basket of summer fruit which some peddler beside the road is trying to sell. To the Lord's question, he can only answer, "It is a basket of summer fruit."

The object of this vision does not present an obvious meaning like those of the first two. Nor is it something which can be a symbolic tool for God to use. God has to supply the key to its meaning, and that key lies in two Hebrew words which sound very much alike. It may even be that in Amos' day they were pronounced exactly the same. Summer fruit is *qăyits*. God's explanation stressed *qēts*, the end: *"The end is coming for my people Israel; I will never pass by them again."*

Amos is in Judah. Yet the heavy burden of the mission God had given him to accomplish lies upon his heart. Perhaps a year has passed. As he makes his way toward Jerusalem for the annual observance of the new year, his thoughts are upon the events of the previous year. The year had gone by quietly. The expected crisis had not come. He would certainly be asked about his prophecies by friends at the festival. Perhaps enemies would jeer at him with jokes about prophets whose words did not come true.

Then comes this vision, and Amos knows that his words had indeed been true. They would yet come to pass in God's own time. He goes on to the festival with determined heart. God had spoken to him again. He would repeat his prophecies and supplement them with the words God had just given him.

As he enters the court of the sanctuary, he is greeted from all sides. His fame, as the prophet who had been banished from Bethel, had spread throughout the land. The people expect a word. Amos finds a convenient spot in a corner of the court. As his countrymen crowd about him, he begins: "Thus the Lord showed me." And he recounts the visions one after another. This is his report concerning his prophetic activity in Israel.

Then a fourth time he begins: "Thus the Lord showed me . . . a basket of summer fruit. Then the Lord said to me, 'The end is coming for my people Israel; I will never pass by them again.'"

It is significant in this vision, as in the third, that the Lord speaks of "my people Israel." One can "feel" the heartbreak of God. The proper setting for this expression is in the words, "You shall be my people and I shall be your God." This was in the assembly of the covenant people. But now God must speak it as he decrees judgment on his people. The words are perfumed with divine pathos.

But the import of the message is nonetheless clear, God's judgment on Israel is being restated and substantiated. The end is sure. This is neither chastisement nor trial. Israel has been weighed and found wanting. The executioner is at the door.

The songs of merriment and carefree folly would change into wails of anguish in that day. The dead would be so many that funeral services with the accustomed mourning would be impossible. Such is the judgment which Israel's sin had made necessary.

This picture of Israel's judgment is broader and deeper than before. The people must face "the end" of all that had made them a people, a kingdom, a nation. Neither in the Northern Kingdom nor in its people, as such, could one look further for the fulfilment of God's election and promise. The speeches in the rest of the chapter are expressions of the deep conviction which this vision produced. They may have been spoken on the occasion of the recital of the visions, or they may have come at other occasions during the succeeding year.

Coming judgments (vv. 4-14).—This chapter may well be understood as a single speech expounding the meaning of "the end" which had been revealed to the prophet.

"Hear this, you who trample upon the needy, and bring the poor of the land to an end." Amos here turns from the prophecy *about* Israel to a direct address to those responsible for the sorry state of affairs which occasioned the judgment. Those designated here are the zealous, greedy, and materialistic businessmen who spurned both the religious symbols and practices of their times and the personal integrity of the poor who worked for them and were their customers. They observed the religious practices of "new moon and sabbath" by not actually doing business. But they could think of nothing else through that day as they impatiently waited for the first moment when they could open their businesses again.

This is the kind of materialistic thinking we find all about us today. People are often much too busy making money to think of the welfare of their souls. If they attend church on Sunday, it is only a form. The Word of God cannot find a place in their thinking and in their lives. It must not be so. There are excellent businessmen who give freely of their time, attention, money, and talents to the work of the Lord. There are those in whose hearts thoughts about God and his will take precedence over their financial and business matters. And many of these are just as successful in business as their colleagues who think of nothing but business. Surely these true Christian businessmen are immeasurably more successful than the others in the matter of living.

The second characteristic which Amos emphasizes is dishonesty. Their impatience to get on with their business is an impatience to get back to their work of cheating and robbing.

This is always a danger. When anyone is wholly absorbed in money and "things," he has no standards by which to judge right or wrong except success. Whatever works is right. Whatever he can get by with is allowed. The only correction for such a way of thinking is through a recognition of divine law and of the worth of human personality.

The third plays upon a phrase already used, "Buy the poor for silver and the needy for a pair of shoes." This seems to refer again to the practices of bribery of the courts, whereby a poor peasant might be declared bankrupt and forced to sell himself into slavery in order to pay his debts. These ambitious exploiters of old knew no limits to their zeal in making money and in gaining power. They trod on men and justice alike without regard.

Wherever they were, in Israel far away or even in Judah, these ought to know that they are the ones who have contributed more than any others to the guilt of Israel. Amos' words carry down the centuries a cry of warning and condemnation upon all who still deal in the same way.

The description of judgment then moves back to a more impersonal description in the third person. We are conscious that Amos is presenting God's message concerning persons who are not present. But the meaning of the prophecies is clear.

One manifestation of the judgment will be the withholding of life-giving conditions from the fields: "Is it because of this that the land does not respond, although every inhabitant mourn with her and her treasured contents flow up like the Nile, and be spread about and irrigate like the Nile of Egypt?" (v. 8). The land is dry and unproductive. Amos' question suggests that it is a judgment of God and is effective, despite ritual rites of mourning and spreading of water as symbolic prayers for rain.[1]

---

[1]*Vision and Prophecy in Amos, op. cit.*, pp. 41-43.

"'On that day,' says the Lord Yahweh, 'I will make the sun go down at noon, and darken the earth in broad daylight.'" The prophecy then goes on to show how this judgment works symbolically as well. What is here pictured as a total eclipse darkens all of life, turning feasting into mourning and joyful songs into lamentations. Amos had said that the day of the Lord would be darkness and not light. He illustrates here what he meant. All of life would be made bitter and barren.

The third characteristic is more original and gripping than the first two: "I will send a famine on the land; not a famine of bread, nor a thirst for water, but of hearing the words of the Lord. They shall wander from sea to sea, and from north to east; they shall run to and fro to seek the word of the Lord, but they shall not find it." (vv. 11-12, RSV).

God's revelation through his prophets is an expression of his grace. One may not take for granted that it will always be there. In that time of judgment, God removes his presence. That is the heaviest judgment that God can lay upon a person or a generation. When God himself is withdrawn, the means by which he usually contacts his people will disappear. No prophet will remain in all the land who can speak in Yahweh's name.

Only when the blessed word is no longer to be heard will the people become seriously interested. Through generations they have silenced the prophets and corrupted other men of God with no concern for the treasure they have destroyed. When it is no longer to be found, they suddenly are frantic to hear it.

This thought is a serious one for our generation to consider. At no time in the history of the world have there been so many churches, so many pulpits, so many Bibles, so many preachers. There are few places in the world where an earnest seeker for the word of God must seek in vain. We find on every hand forces at work to close the mouths of the preachers, to close the churches, to limit evangelism, to destroy and discredit the Bible. It must be a serious thought for us as well that this time of freedom to proclaim and to hear God's Word may not last forever. We, too, must "work, for the night cometh when no man can work."

Amos brings his prophecy to a close with a picture of the fate of those who have put their trust on the local divinities of Samaria, Dan, and Beersheba (and no doubt other places as well). There is no test of the validity of religious faith like that of crisis and trouble. In such times, only a faith which has changed all of life into one dependent upon the grace and power of God alone will be sufficient for that hour. All false religions and all unfounded faith will fade and perish in that hour, just as the worshipers of false gods are pictured as doing in this prophecy.

5

The Day of Yahweh

The Fifth Period (9:1-15)

Death and resurrection (vv. 1-6).—The final vision does not follow the pattern familiar in the other four. It is a form known in other accounts (cf. Isa. 6). But it is less a prophecy than an account of seeing the Lord already at work in bringing the judgment upon Israel.

It might be possible to date this prophecy in the years in which the Assyrians broke in upon Israel and lay siege around Samaria. Amos might have lived so long, and this might well be his description of the fulfilment of his prophecies.

However, it seems much more suitable to connect this scene with the earthquake referred to in the superscription which came just two years to the day after Amos had been expelled from Bethel. The reasons for this choice were presented in chapter 1. It has sometimes been suggested that the vision in which Isaiah knew his call occurred at the same time.

We may reconstruct the events in this way. As the second anniversary of his banishment comes, Amos makes his way to a Judean sanctuary (perhaps even Jerusalem) to observe the New Year. It would have been natural for the thoughts of his ministry in the north to be heavy upon his spirit in those days.

Perhaps he even repeated the accounts of his visions, as he had the year before.

Then, just as the ceremonies for the New Year reached their peak, Amos stood with the great crowd, eagerly awaiting the great ritual acts. Instead of ritual, the earth began to quiver, the pillars of the temple tottered down into the mass of the people. The altar shook and was damaged. Fourteen miles away at Bethel the results were equally disastrous.

Amos stood with open eyes, seeing in it all the beginning of God's judgment, just as he had proclaimed it .

"I saw the Lord standing beside the altar, and he said: 'Smite the capitals until the thresholds shake, and scatter them on the heads of all the people' " (v. 1, RSV).

This was none other than God who commanded and who acted in the earthquake. He was beginning to act in judgment against his people. But it should be plain that this was only a beginning. God would carry his judgment on to the bitter end.

"What is left of them I will slay with the sword; not one of them shall flee away, not one of them shall escape."

The judgments which God had determined would be fulfilled in every detail. There can be no thought of hiding from the judgment of the Lord—in earth, Sheol, or heaven.

The messages of the last two periods of the prophet's ministry had made it abundantly clear that God had "set his eyes upon them for evil and not for good." God is the Lord. If he cannot be the Lord of salvation for his people, he must be the Lord of judgment and destruction. Neither in the one case nor the other is it possible to escape his sovereign rule.

No unconditional election (v. 7).—" 'Are you not like the Ethiopians to me, O people of Israel?' says the Lord. 'Did I not bring up Israel from the land of Egypt, and the Philistines from Caphtor and the Syrians from Kir?' "

There are two significant statements concerning election in Amos. The first is in 3:2, where he acknowledges Israel's election but goes on to show that this is the very basis for God's judgment.

In chapter 9, he again moves to answer the objection that God would not deal with his elect people in this way. His questioner seems to have objected that this would make Israel no different to God than any other nation, whereas in reality God had sealed his own relation to Israel through his wonderful deliverance from Egypt. Because God had arbitrarily intervened on behalf of his people and had confirmed his relation to Israel through the Exodus, he could not act in judgment, as Amos had claimed.

God's word which Amos speaks is intended to harshly denounce an attitude of presumption. The people think of Yahweh in terms of a national God who is so bound to his people that he must act only in their interest. Amos thinks of God as the Lord of all the world, marvelous and majestic in his free sovereignty. But God is definitely related to all the great migrations of history. His purposes may be different with each one, but the fact that God controlled Israel's march out of Egypt and into Canaan does not give Israel the right to insist on his favor through all time. Quite the reverse is true. It does give God the basis for insisting that Israel must be true to him, for he has bought her through the action of his free grace.

These two statements in Amos are designed to combat a common attitude of bland presumption on the part of the people. They are not contradictory but complementary in their statements which try to correct the false ideas held by Israelites of their election.

This doctrine of election is the key to an understanding of Old Testament or biblical theology. No understanding of the doctrines of salvation or of judgment is possible except within the framework of this doctrine of election. Unless this election is seen within the broad bounds of Mosaic ethical monotheism, the biblical pattern will continue to elude us.

This is clear in Amos. For Amos, Yahweh is the Creator of all the world and of all men. He is the ruling Lord over all men and nations, and this rule may be seen in the events of history. But it is equally clear that Amos knows that the basis of God's rule is moral. His will is moral, and his acts are intended to accomplish his will.

It is in the dialectic posed by these two great features that God's way with Israel is to be understood. He is the free Lord of all, so that there is nothing which binds his freedom of action. On the other hand, his will is holy and moral. In accordance with his will he has made a plan to deal with the world. This plan is one by which he will make for himself a people. The heart of this plan is the election of Israel and his covenant with her. The results of this way of action within the covenant and on the basis of election are salvation and judgment. These last two go together and cannot be separated. Neither is to be presumed, for no one can force God's grace. Yet toward those who are truly his people, God is invariably faithful to save. Toward those who stand against God, his judgment is equally predictable. Amos' theology may be summed up in this way.

Destruction of the kingdom—sifting for the people (vv. 8-10).—"Behold, the eyes of the Lord God are upon the sinful kingdom, and I will destroy it from the surface of the ground."

In these words the prophecies of judgment in Amos reach their peak. Amos picks up the statement of verse 4, which had been interrupted by the doxology and the cry concerning Israel's election. But now he is careful to make explicit the object of this complete destruction.

It is the "sinful kingdom," or perhaps better translated "illegal kingdom," which has to be completely destroyed. Its very existence—including the ruling house with its supporting group of land-grabbing nobility and the national sanctuaries, whose principal purpose had been the preservation and well-being of the kingdom—was under judgment.

From the beginning of its existence this kingdom had been a rebellion against God's order in the Davidic dynasty. From the beginning its sanctuaries had been opposed to the established and legitimate worship in Jerusalem. None of the many rulers had brought the people back to the true worship of Yahweh or to a unification with the rulers and sanctuary which God had established. The kingdom was illegal and unauthorized from the beginning, says Amos. God must destroy it in order to achieve his ultimate purpose for Israel.

But what of the people? Although the sinful kingdom must be destroyed, "I will not utterly destroy the house of Jacob," says the Lord. "For lo, I will command, and shake the house of Israel among all the nations as one shakes with a sieve, but no pebble shall fall from the earth. All the sinners of my people shall die by the sword, who say, 'Evil shall not overlook or meet us.'"

When we read these words in this way, noting the conscious contrast between kingdom and people, there is no reason to think of the contradiction which so many commentaries see here. Although the kingdom must be destroyed, the people will only be sifted. The people are elect, not the kingdom.

But the people will not simply escape. The heavy hand of judgment will fall upon them. No more apt figure could be found for the judgments which were to befall Israel, and later Judah, than that of a sieve. Shaken and scattered among all the nations was to be the fate of this people.

From such a judgment there will be no "escape." No one can presume to have a pass which will make it unnecessary for him to be shaken in the sieve. And through this sifting "all the sinners of my people" will be destroyed. All of their self-assurance, bred in them by false religion and self-deceit, will be of no help. They will die, but what of the rest?

"Hope in Amos (vv. 11-15).—" 'In that day I will raise up the booth of David that is fallen and repair its breaches, and raise up its ruins, and rebuild it as in the days of old; that they may possess the remnant of Edom and all the nations who are called by my name,' says the Lord who does this."

These last few verses present a dramatic contrast to the rest of the book, which breathes dark, foreboding prophecies of destruction. These lines bring assurances of salvation and hope. Most modern commentaries cast them aside as later additions. They say that Amos was a prophet of judgment, not of hope. But how do they know? We have already taken a careful look at the warm, tender side of Amos. We have seen that his character is not so starkly simple as to be described by a single word.

So, is it possible that Amos did utter these words? Do they belong to his thinking, to his understanding of God's will and ways?

A careful examination of the verses shows that there is nothing here which Amos *could* not have said. Further, the typical motifs of exilic eschatology are entirely lacking. This is not the place for a full argument of the point. Suffice it to say that the words might very well have been his. I take them as original. If so, what are we to say of the hope expressed in them? Does it fit into the rest of Amos' thought?

First, we must note that the hope is closely connected with the coming "day of Yahweh." This concept is well known to the people. They thought of it in two parts—a day of judgment on all the enemies of Yahweh (i.e. on the enemies of Israel) and a day of rejoicing, of victory, of establishment in prosperity and peace for the *remnant* (i.e. Israel). Amos quarreled basically with the popular view at one point only. He agreed that it would be a day of judgment on the enemies of Yahweh (1:2-3). But he could not agree to the proposition that "the remnant equals Israel." Israel must be punished, too (2:6-16; 3:2; 3:12; 5:18). Amos never questioned the fact that there would be *a remnant*. But that leaves the question, "Who then is the remnant?"

The last verses give the answer. The first part of the answer stresses the promises to the Davidic line and the place that line will have in the blessed remnant. What Amos is saying is that *the remnant* will be the restored Davidic kingdom with all of the territory included in it which had been promised (or claimed) for it. This is the equivalent of saying that the key to the blessed remnant is Judah, the little mountain kingdom.

Surely people in Judah must have long since asked themselves when Yahweh would act to make good his promises to the Davidic house? When would he punish the rebellious Northern Kingdom for throwing off the reign of the divinely chosen line (cf. 9:8a)? Amos belonged to this group. His message for Israel is that the destruction of the Northern Kingdom is part of a positive program to achieve Yahweh's purpose. The hope for Israel lies in being finally reunited with Judah. This judgment will make that possible.

The breaches and ruins which are referred to are dramatic illustrations of the poor state of Judah. Broken in pieces through the separation of the Northern Kingdom, torn apart and weakened by frequent wars with this kingdom and others of the surrounding kingdoms, she must at this time have been nothing more than a ruin of the glory that was Solomon's. One does not need to look for the days of the Babylonian exile for the historical setting which fits these words.

When this great vista of the promised Davidic empire, once having belonged to David and having had "Yahweh's name called over it" as a symbol of his ownership and rule, is contrasted with the "sinful kingdom" of the previous section, we have the proper setting for understanding Amos' judgment and his picture of salvation.

"Behold, the days are coming," says the Lord. Note that "the days" stands in contrast to the previous "on that day." The latter is the "day of Yahweh" in which God will act in judgment and in salvation. These days now referred to are the period which will result. It is within the conditions of the fully established Davidic kingdom that God's old promises of abiding and undisturbed prosperity within their own land may be fulfilled for God's people, Israel.

The elements of this prophecy are not distinctive to Amos. Every element belonged to the common hope and dream of Israel, which is much older than he is. There is no reason why Amos could not have said it. But Amos' great contribution lies rather in defining the conditions under which this might be fulfilled.

This great prosperity is characterized by a rapid succession of seasons and the resulting fertility of the land. In it God will "restore the fortunes of his people." This phrase, which is composed of two Hebrew words which sound much alike, used to be translated "bring back the exiles." Now it is understood as a parallel, known in other Semitic languages, which simply means to "turn the course of things," usually of fate, from good to bad or vice versa. In those days Israel's fortunes, which had been so bad for so long, were to turn so that all would be good and work in her favor.

The final promises have to do with permanence and stability in the land. Poor little Palestine has known little of this in its long history. Wars and raiding tribesmen made existence perilous in those days, just as it is through much of that country today. These days would bring a stability and permanence in life unknown before.

Finally, it would bring the fulfilment of a promise which was as old as Abraham, that this land would be firmly and unquestionably theirs. This promise of "the land of rest," as Joshua calls it, became a figure in the Old Testament times for the permanence and surety of a people with God in their midst and blessing them.

This last description is not made in the spiritual or theological terms which may be found elsewhere. Amos is not concerned to form this anew. He has been concerned to show God's will and God's action which would lead to this goal and to interpret them for his day. This continues to be the task of God's spokesmen.

Part II

THE FAITH OF AMOS

6

Who Yahweh Is

Instead of dealing with the text on a passage-by-passage basis, this chapter and the next survey Amos' major doctrinal teachings. These doctrines lie at the very heart of Old Testament teaching. In the work of the prophets from Amos on, the central beliefs of Old Testament theology were revived and applied in an unparalleled way.

The content of the prophets' teaching was not new. But the force and consistency of the faith that applied it to life and history was new and unique. This in turn placed ancient truth in a very different and pertinent light.

Amos' doctrinal foundation, like any good theology, was built on basic convictions about God, about man, and about the area of their interaction.

The Sovereignty of Yahweh

No one can read the words of Amos without being impressed anew with the majestic and terrible character of divine sovereignty and man's freedom to determine his own way and to act on it. For Amos, Yahweh was the great, sovereign God who ruled over all things, whose decisions and actions could not be controlled through ritual hocus-pocus. Neither could his favor be curried by petty bribery nor his judgment turned aside by a show of man's futile force.

Yahweh rules the forces of the universe without challenge. He fixed the earth in its place and gave it stability. He established regularity of the seasons and the stars. His absolute rule here is all that preserves order and unity in the universe. His power and faithfulness make it possible to speak about "laws of nature." He brings the rain and he withholds it. He brings the light of day through the sun, and he can darken it at noonday if he so decides. The various passages of the hymn referred to earlier praise Yahweh for his sovereign control of the world and all its powers and forces (4:12-13; 5:8-9; 9:5-6).

Ancient heathen people also believed that the gods controlled the world and the universe. But they understood the changes and discrepancies as coming from struggles between different gods. Amos believed, and Israel believed, that Yahweh ruled there alone in sovereign majesty. This doctrine does not solve all the problems the human mind faces in this area, but it remains today the basic point of departure for the Christian's atttiude toward nature, the world, and the universe.

In Amos' visions, Yahweh appears as the one who controls the destructive elements of nature (7:1-6; 8:8b-9). This comes from the basic tenet of faith that Yahweh is the ruler of all the world. All power and control of nature belongs to him.

So it is with the "fire" which Yahweh will place in the courts and fortresses of the judged nations. This "fire" is not set by men. It is "fire from heaven," a cosmic fire, a kind of divine lightning which accomplishes the judgment of Yahweh (1:4,7,10,12,14; 2:2,5; 7:4).

This understanding of God's work in nature is not to be generalized. Every natural catastrophe is not a judgment. But every catastrophe can be a reminder that man is not Lord of all. Even as man expands his range of understanding and control in nature, God alone is really "in control."

It is equally clear that Amos recognized Yahweh's sovereignty over history. Men and nations move at his will. The judgments over various nations in the first two chapters make this unmistakably plain (1:3 to 2:16). But that is not all. Yahweh will raise up a great nation (obviously Assyria) to carry out his judgment against Israel (6:14).

It is not merely in judgment that God's control is exercised over the nations. The great migrations which formed the warp and woof of Near Eastern life were under his control. "Did I not bring up Israel from the land of Egypt, and the Philistines from Caphtor and the Syrians from Kir?" (9:7, RSV). The completeness of his control is shown in the promise that in the judgment which will fall on Israel none can escape (9:1-4).

The very ways in which God's relation to Israel is shown, however, point to a different relation than that found in the natural world. Here it is more like a shepherd herding his sheep—a whistle here, a slap there, which keeps the herd moving in the right direction. In history God is dealing with men and groups of men to whom he has granted considerable autonomy. They do not always do what God wants and much of God's work is taken up with correction and judgment. But when all else is considered it is he, not they, who have determined the direction which history should take, and he will certainly determine its goal and end.

God's full sovereignty gives him a freedom of self-determination which we would do well to grasp anew in our day. It is in the exercise of this sovereign freedom that the "election of Israel" is to be understood. God was free to choose whomever he liked. He chose Israel (3:2). Because he did this in complete exercise of free grace, he is also free to make his own demands and to cut off the people when they do not meet his demands. He is under no obligation to the people. Quite the contrary. The people are under obligation to him (2:9-11). God is not bound up within his order, within his law; he is sovereign over all, including his own order of things. This leaves room for the possibility of grace, to which we have already referred.

Only as God is completely sovereign can he truly be God. The exercise of grace and election, just as much as judgment, is otherwise unthinkable. The God Amos served was such a sovereign, and "the God and Father of our Lord Jesus Christ" is, too.

Amos' understanding of God's unlimited sovereignty or lordship was not simply tied to the great areas of the world and to history in general. It was also very personally and individually known to Amos. The mighty God of all the universe, the wielder of the determining forces of history, was known to deal quite personally with individual men. He called men out from the mass of the group to repent, to choose between salvation and judgment. It is true that the general background of Amos' understanding (and of the people as well, for that matter) was one of social solidarity. Amos does not challenge this in principle, and most of his prophecy is addressed to the people as such without singling out one or another. But one cannot utter the challenges to turn, to change, the plea for personal decisions in the face of God's word without having already pulled away from the bonds of social solidarity as they were generally understood.

Amos is basically not a theoretical individualist. He does not teach individualism. But he understood his own relation to God, his call, and his conversations with God in quite personal and individual terms (2:11; 7:14-15). God had spoken to him, as he was accustomed to do to the prophets. He had called him out to do his work. He was not a representative of the group. He was the representative of God alone. As a result, he could speak quite intimately and personally to God, calling him "Lord" (vv. 1-9). God was his Lord. As a result, he could call on others to recognize him as their Lord.

The issue of the individual or the group as the main focus for Christian thinking continues today. For Amos, "Israel" the group was the major and central focus, even as "the church of Jesus

Christ" must be for the Christian today. But Amos did not allow this to set aside the free access of God to the individual and the basic responsibility of the individual to God. In a real sense, neither the true Israel nor the true church can consist of other than those who are individually committed persons. This was the basic meaning of the covenant in Israel—in its ancient practice each Israelite man entered its privileges only on a personal commitment of himself to its provisions. God speaks to and calls individuals today to become a part of, and to serve in, his church. When they enter they cross a line where individualism is no longer proper. Even so, God goes on calling individuals for the good of the church.

There is no clear expression of a doctrine of theoretical monotheism in Amos as is found in Deutero-Isaiah. Amos is not a theologian; he is a prophet. But it is the proclamation of the complete sovereignty of God as Amos does it which makes the theological formulation of pure monotheism possible and necessary. Amos does not hesitate to ascribe divine power to Yahweh.

Moral Character and Purpose

The words "justice" and "righteousness" appear so often in Amos that everyone is familiar with the description of him as "the prophet of social justice." But the power of his preaching on this subject has its source neither in his repetitive insistence nor in his keen observation of the ways of men.

The source of his concern lies in his recognition that Yahweh has been revealed to be moral in his own character and that his purpose and will cannot be understood apart from fundamental ethical considerations. Amos has little time for abstract thinking about God. He understands him as a moral being whose judgments are made on moral grounds. God's requirements of ethical practice apply to all people. His will is summed up in the cry, "Let justice roll down like waters, and righteousness like an everflowing stream!" (5:24).

Amos' emphasis on the ethical character of Yahweh was not a new idea in Israel. The covenant made at Sinai had stressed in the so-called Ten Commandments that God wanted total commitment and ethical behavior from the people. Of course, the covenant included provisions for worship, but the basic provisions pointed to the people's life.

As time went on, interest in the ritual observances increased and compromises led the people as well as the rulers to forget the awesome, ethical imperatives on which the covenant was based. They also forgot the genuine confrontation with God, which covenant ceremonies were intended to make possible.

Now Amos comes with his attacks on the ritual places, acts, and personnel. Amid vituperative attacks stand calls to positive action: "Seek me and live!" (v. 4) "Seek good instead of evil!" (v. 14).

Yahweh's demands for righteousness and justice are so heavy that they do not make room for persons with other goals in life to share his fellowship. This has nothing to do with the legalistic keeping of specific provisions of the Law in later Judaism. It refers to a basic commitment to the same standards of life that are Yahweh's and which he has revealed in the covenant. If one is unable to keep them, repentance and sacrifice can pave the way for forgiveness. But a lack of commitment to them is truly intolerable.

Amos' emphasis on the ethical character of Yahweh does not introduce a completely new idea into the theological thought of Israel. But his interpretation of the judgments to come as being caused purely and simply through the breach of ethical behavior (injustice, and so on) on the part of the people was certainly new to his listeners. That judgment on the people should spring basically from the ethical motives of Yahweh is the great contribution of Amos to Old Testament theology. He might even be called the prophet of ethical causality. It is his recognition and proclamation of the fact that Yahweh is to be known essentially for his "absolute ethical will" that stands out so clearly in his prophecy.

For a people who, like most others in the Near East, had come to think of the basic requirements of Yahweh in purely ritualistic terms, this must have come like a bolt from the blue. That they should be condemned for the very acts of worship which they thought the most pious things about them must have been a source of indignation to all. That God was primarily interested in the way they treated the poor and humble people of the land, that he was more concerned with how they acted toward each other than with how they ostensibly treated him was a complete surprise, a blow at the very foundation of their life, as they understood it.

What Amos is saying is that the basic character of God can be known. The mighty God who exercises unlimited sovereign power and authority does not deal with men without principle and character. He acts according to his basic character. That character is moral and ethical to the core. He demands justice and right from men, for he is just and righteous. His purposes in the world are ethically motivated. He wants justice and right to prevail. His judgment will be based on this principle.

The basic theological concept of the Old Testament is rightly called *ethical monotheism*. In the statement of principles of the theology of ethical monotheism, Amos must be reckoned a place of supreme importance. It is he who so plainly states that justice toward one's fellows is properly to be reckoned as a central feature of religious faith. James echoes this concern for the welfare of people: "Pure religion and undefiled before God and the Father is this, To visit the fatherless and widows in their affliction" (1:27).

7

Man Under God

Amos took man seriously because he had learned that God was serious in his concern for man. The statements which can be made about Amos' view of man all grow from his basic concept of God and from his experiences with him.

Sin.—As Amos looked on men about him one fact overshadowed all else. It was the fact of sin. He could not escape it. His thinking is between the poles of God's purpose and man's sin.

Amos' point of departure in thinking of sin is not in some high concept of the state of man. Sin is not seen in terms of a high immortality which man was too weak or foolish to grasp. Nor is it pictured as a quality in man which he cannot escape, although he does recognize that this generation had become so used to sin that they did not "know how to do right" (3:10).

For Amos, sin was primarily an offense against God's sovereignty. It was rebellion, as the word used so often in the first chapters shows. But this rebellion appeared in unethical behavior toward one's fellowmen. The very man who piously fulfilled all the ritual ceremonies directed toward God was guilty of rebellion in not doing God's will in everyday life. It was a case of those who say "Lord! Lord" but do not do what the Lord has commanded them (Matt. 7:21).

Amos knew that God's will was essentially moral, yet he knew that it was also redemptive. His message called for Israel to recognize her sin, to repent, and to seek God. It was not simply the sin itself which was bad. It was worse that the people did not even recognize their own sin. The deeds they thought most pious were their most serious rebellions.

This fact of sin Amos observed in all the nations. God's ethical will was not to be limited to his own people. It applied to all. As God was Lord of history, so his will must apply to all peoples. Amos presumes a certain ethical sense of right and wrong that can properly be applied to all peoples in spite of the lack of specific revelation of something like the covenant.

But sin was most clearly perceived and defined in Israel. For God had revealed to Israel "what is good." In addition, this had been given to Israel in a setting which mediated the actual presence and blessing of God. Israel, to whom the mighty and holy God himself had come to dwell, had a much graver responsibility. Israel knew how holy and terrible God was, and she had been clearly told that for her to be "his people" and he "their God," the conditions of the covenant had to be met. When she flagrantly ignored God's requirements for justice and interpreted righteousness purely in terms of ritual acts, she was inviting doom.

All men had sinned, but any who turned and sought God would find him and be found of him. This was Amos' deepest conviction.

Freedom.—We have noted the particular emphasis Amos places on God's sovereign freedom. His emphasis on man's freedom should not be overlooked.

Throughout his speeches Amos pleads with the people to repent and seek God, even when his main theme is the opposite. This reflects a basic conviction that the people are free to repent and to seek their God (5:4-6) at any time. Only after the bitter judgment is the situation changed (8:12).

These freedoms are not understood as inherent qualities in man, nor as rights which he has because he is man. As God is free, he has ordained that men shall be free to do his will. God has acted not only in the beginning but repeatedly in every life to make it possible for a man to do his will. This corresponds to his double will to obedience and redemption.

Amos pleads for men to exercise these basic freedoms to do right and to seek God. These are rights which are denied no man. After all, they are basic to all other rights or freedoms that men may seek anywhere.

Justice.—Amos is known as the prophet of social justice. It is well that a study of his view of man emphasizes this word. Men had a right to justice from their fellowmen because God had willed it so (2:6-7; 3:9d). Justice forms the basis of human society as God had ordained it. Where it cannot be had, neither order nor God can be at home.

But the prophet is not content to cry out for the rights of justice. Far more often he is extolling the responsibility which all men have under God, to provide justice to all men no matter what their status. The application of this principle is a growing thing in the Old Testament. First applied only to Israelites among themselves, it came to be applied to "sojourners and strangers within their gates." There can be no doubt of its intended ultimate universal application. That dominant groups in later Judaism did not realize these universal goals is one of the tragedies of history, paralleled only by Christianity's own frequent lapses in this regard. However these may be, the direct revelation of God in the Scriptures is clear. Justice is every believer's responsibility.

Amos was not a leader of mobs, seeking their rights, although this may be a legitimate activity. He was a preacher who took seriously his duty to preach an announcement of judgment and a call to repentance to those who were perfectly capable of "doing justly" if they decided to do so.

To the very ones who controlled the devious machinery of injustice in the land, Amos cried: "Hate evil, and love good, and establish justice in the gate" (5:15), and "Let justice roll down like waters, and righteousness like an everflowing stream" (v. 24). He was concerned with more than pious resolutions or statements of purpose. He wanted more than legalistic fulfilment of the letter of laws which might be antiquated in their provisions. He wanted a basic commitment to being just, honest, fair, and right to every person, because that is what God is and that is what he insists that his people be.

The heaviest emphasis on this doctrine in Amos falls in his judgments against those who have failed in this responsibility. God's own judgment falls on them because they have spurned this elemental law. And it falls on the sanctuaries and royal house because they have allowed such circumstances to exist.

Revelation.—One should not miss the clear statements in Amos that God has revealed himself and his will to his people. Over and over ring out the words, "Thus says the Lord." This is a prophetic formula. But it is more. It is a testimony to Amos' understanding of the directness with which God was appealing to men through him. His bold declaration of his authority to prophecy (7:14-16) carried the same emphasis.

One of the signs of God's patience and care for Israel has been his repeated sending of prophets to her, even though they were rejected ever and again (2:11-12). Amos even understood it as a clear principle that God always announced and interpreted his doing through his prophets (3:7-8). And finally, one of the darkest judgments which would be given to Israel on the day of the Lord's visitation would be the silence of prophecy (8:11-12).

Although all of Amos' expressions concerning revelation have dealt with prophecy, our eyes should not be blind to the implications concerning other means of revelation. His sharp ethical judgments concerning the sins of the people take for granted a knowledge and understanding of God's law. Such law is not learned through the prophet. It is rather to be heard through the priest in the sanctuary. It seems that both priests and sanctuaries had been lax in this matter in the Northern Kingdom.

God's word was something quite personal and real to Amos. It was at the same time the most precious and the most important thing he knew. His preaching reflected this conviction.

Election.—Amos deals briefly with that unique Old Testament doctrine that God had chosen Israel to be his own people and to fulfil a peculiar mission for him. He does not use the words most frequently picked to express it, nor does he try to give it direct expression. Rather he moves to correct misconceptions arising from it.

His first point (3:2) is that election heightens responsibility. Rather than conferring privileged sanctuary from judgment, election makes punishment for her failure all the more severe. God had chosen Israel in order to walk and live with her. The intimacy of this relation should have prepared her as an ideal witness and servant. Her unwillingness to fulfil the goals of election made her liable to heavier judgment. Election is for service,

His second direct reference (9:6) has a double reference. Her senses of unique calling and experience in the Exodus had led Israel to the false assumptions that God had had nothing to do with other nations and that this historical experience had committed God to them irrevocably. Amos refutes this directly with the assertion that God is the Lord of all history. He leads, guides, and works with all nations, not just Israel. God's election gave Israel the unique privilege of service not accorded other peoples, but it did not entitle her to presumption.

Amos insists that belief in election must be held within an understanding of the universal rule and purpose of God. Israel was called to play an important part in that drama, but she was by no means the only player on the stage. Amos equally insists that election must be understood in terms of a covenant which spells out the terms of her service for God.

A great expositor has said of this teaching: "Religion is no insurance against doom, no mere atonement and escape from consequences. . . . Religion is only opportunity—the greatest moral opportunity which men have, and which if they violate nothing remains for them but a certain fearful looking forward unto judgment."[1]

Covenant.—Some scholars have maintained that Amos makes no reference to covenant. Like election, it is true that he avoids the normal language, but a very cursory reading of the book cannot avoid the impression that Amos' thought is full of the covenant and its forms.

The simple expressions "my people" and "your God" are drawn directly from the covenant.

The Mosaic covenant is based on a careful balancing of promise and demand from God. This contractual agreement calls for settlement and renewal from time to time. Such renewals are recorded in the Old Testament. They review the history of the relations of God and Israel, record God's faithfulness and Israel's sins. Upon a prayer of repentance and appropriate sacrifices, God forgives and renews the covenant on the basis of Israel's new commitment of herself to the terms of covenant.

Amos presumes this situation throughout. Judgment, as he pictures it, is covenant judgment. But there is no sign of repentance or recommitment from Israel. Thus forgiveness is impossible and the judgment must be carried out.

Election within the covenant is always understood to be conditioned on response in commitment and obedience. It is never unconditioned. This is evidently the source of Amos' understanding of both.

Society.—Amos' teachings on justice presuppose certain clear ideas of Israelite society. He thinks of Israel's existence as being internally based on a common commitment to the covenant and

---

[1] G. A. Smith, *The Book of the Twelve Prophets* (rev. ed., Garden City: Doubleday, Doran & Co., 1929), I, 145-46.

the laws of God. This is what makes possible her strength and unity as a people.

It was a society in which all men are free and equal because they all stood directly "under God." It was the duty of each man to see to it that justice existed for all, especially those who could not maintain their own rights, such as the widows and the orphans. Each was responsible for the welfare of all.

A more democratic system could hardly be imagined. Yet Amos found that it had been corrupted in his time and society was rotten throughout. He placed the principle blame on those institutions which were primarily responsible for teaching the people the law of God—the sanctuaries and that institution which had usurped the democratic duties of the populace at large —the monarchy.

History.—History, like society, Amos viewed in terms of God's work in it and rule over it. History shows the movements and plans of nations and rulers—under God. This is the great place in which God works out his purposes. At his command the pieces move across the board fulfilling his great design.

Yet this is not a puppet theater with the people jerked on strings. There is need for decision and responsible action. God in many ways—calling, judging, coaxing, ordaining—nudges the pieces toward his determined goals. The heathen know nothing of this. Israel is privileged to know her calling, her destiny, and her judgment.

Judgment.—Amos has perhaps more to say about judgment than any other one subject. He understands judgment to be on the basis of an ethical standard. His vision of the plumb line had made that clear enough. But this emphasis on an ethical stand-ard is not enough to explain Amos' view. There is something else which gives his conception both its severity and its particular limitations. He views judgment within the realm of election. Because this is his elect people, God will bring his judgment to bear upon them for their sin (3:2).

Amos seems to think about the accomplishment of this judgment in three different ways. God's judgments are intended to chastise his people and turn them toward a life of justice and righteousness through repentance (4:6-11). Then God's judgment is seen as destruction of the kingdom, the sanctuaries, and all else which resists his will (3:12; 9:1-8a). And finally, judgment appears to him as God's means of sifting and purifying his people (9:8b-10). Through all these we can see that judgment is one of the tools which God uses to accomplish his purposes.

Salvation.—It has often been said that no doctrine of salvation exists in Amos. But this is certainly a radical misinterpretation which overlooks many items. It is true that Amos' preaching had to be directed more toward judgment than salvation. But from the few positive turns in his messages we may learn some things.

Amos' emphasis upon sin as the violation of a moral standard might be thought of as implying that salvation must be earned through ethical merit. This is not true. Verse 13 of chapter 5 makes this plain. He urged the people to repent and do right with the hope that "*it may be* that the Lord will be gracious." The free grace of God cannot be coerced or earned. For Amos, salvation is by grace alone.

Amos preaches the necessity of repentance for salvation (vv. 4-6). Sinners who continue in their sin cannot be saved. For them there can only be judgment. Grace is for those who will repent and seek Yahweh.

Behind the words of Amos lies the assumption that God has had a purpose for Israel, that he has acted on this purpose (2:9-11), and that his salvation for them will be in line with this purpose (9:11-15). Salvation, like judgment, comes within the framework of God's election and his purpose. For this reason, descriptions of salvation may be made in terms of a remnant which survives the sifting of judgment as the restored booth of David.

Eschatology.—Eschatology is the doctrine of last things. Amos has much to say about "the day of Yahweh," which is one of the terms used to describe that last time. Does he have a teaching which we can take over to form our own ideas of the last days? The answer must be both yes and no.

In general terms, Amos understands "the day" as that time when God will decisively intervene in the affairs of history to set things straight and establish his own reign. It was not to be simply one day of the festival, as many of his fellow citizens understood it. Rather, it would be that decisive day in history in which the imagery of the festival ritual would take on historical form.

There is no hint that the intervention which he predicts would mean the end of all things. Quite the contrary. A true eschatology in the sense of the doctrine of the last things of time and history came into existence long after Amos. But when it did appear, it used the teachings of the prophets like Amos to expound its doctrines.

In God's will Amos recognizes that constant sure work of God which was symbolized by his promise to David, as well as the covenant theology which was the basis of his pronouncement of justice. Not only responsibility and judgment but also "the sure mercies of David" (9:11) will determine the end.

Conclusion

This is Amos as he comes to us from the pages of his books. We often feel disappointed that we do not find things in his message which we would like to find. It is not the kind of book that one reads again and again as a devotional book. Nor was Amos the kind of preacher one would invite to young people's conferences to bring the inspiring devotional lectures. The book does seem to fall short of the peak of some others.

"Yet it is exhilarating. How clearly he puts first things first. There is a lift about this man, a freedom, a throwing off of ordinary human hesitations that acts as a tonic to our sluggish spirits. Amos lives in a vaster world, where wealth and splendor count for nothing, where kings seem small, where the power of the powerful is contemptible and the only things worthy of honor are justice and purity and truth, where what God thinks is the supreme question. He is one of the great emancipated spirits of the race. And he is one of the most passionate champions of the poor. Whenever men have gone to the Bible for encouragement in the long struggle for the liberation of the underprivileged, they have found it chiefly in Amos and in those successors whom he deeply influenced—Isaiah and Micah."[2]

---

[2]Fleming James, *Personalities of the Old Testament* (New York: Charles Scribner's Sons, 1939), p. 228.